PELICAN BOOKS

Lives of the Great Composers

VOLUME II

(A91)

PELICAN BOOKS

LIVES OF THE
GREAT COMPOSERS
II

BEETHOVEN AND THE ROMANTICS

BEETHOVEN by Peter Latham
BERLIOZ by Edwin Evans
CHOPIN by Herbert Hughes
LISZT by Ralph Hill
MENDELSSOHN by Max Pirani
MOUSSORGSKY by M. D. Calvocoressi
ROSSINI by Francis Toye
SCHUBERT by William Glock
SCHUMANN by A. E. F. Dickinson
WEBER by Edwin Evans

edited by A. L. Bacharach

PUBLISHED BY
PENGUIN BOOKS
WEST DRAYTON MIDDLESEX ENGLAND
245 FIFTH AVENUE NEW YORK U.S.A.

First Published 1935
Published in Pelican Books 1943
Reprinted NOVEMBER 1947

MADE AND PRINTED IN GREAT BRITAIN
FOR PENGUIN BOOKS LTD., BY WYMAN & SONS LIMITED
LONDON, FAKENHAM AND READING

EDITOR'S PREFACE

This book and its two companions are about the lives of composers, not about their compositions—a ridiculous division of the indivisible, you may well observe. As reasonably attempt to write a life of Shakespeare and leave out the plays or of Dalton and leave out the atomic theory. Be that as it may, we have attempted to show you the man, explained, if you will, by his creative work, where that has been necessary and possible, rather than the work explained by the man.

In the first volume are gathered together biographies of men who lived in the sixteenth, seventeenth and eighteenth centuries, from Palestrina, who was born in 1525 or 1526, to Haydn, who lived longer than most of our subjects and by dying in 1809—at the good age of 77—carried over the pre-classical and classical period of music into the nineteenth century. The artificiality of a purely arbitrary division into three volumes—as of all such divisions in a living and developing art—is emphatically brought home to us when we recall that Haydn was already eighteen years old in the year of Bach's death, and yet he died only four years before the birth of Verdi and Wagner, both of whom are subjects of biographies in the third volume!

The second volume has been called—for want of a better description—'Beethoven and the Romantics,' a title that, admittedly, begs more questions than it answers. For this title the Editor takes full responsibility and all the blame; the contributors are entirely innocent. In years, the volume covers a much shorter time than does volume one, but not by any means a less pregnant period. From the birth of Beethoven in 1770 to the death of Liszt in 1886, music had undergone changes and developments that must be heard to be believed.

Volume three, 'Brahms, Wagner and their Contemporaries,' carries us from 1813 to the death of Elgar in 1934, covering in years a period very little longer than that of volume two. With perhaps the exception of Debussy, who was in more ways than one 'an end in himself,' the composers included in this volume can claim to have been consolidating and exploiting the advances made by their romantic predecessors rather than breaking lances and idols. It is strange to read to-day of the wild controversies that ranged round the music-dramas of Richard Wagner in a world that knew Berlioz and Liszt, to say nothing of the later Beethoven and the early Verdi.

Nevertheless, the distribution of our subjects between volumes two and three is one that the Editor, for his part, while taking full responsibility, does not really attempt to justify on grounds of logic, aesthetics, or history. And to those who suggest that it is absurd to place Moussorgsky and Liszt in Volume Two, while Tchaikovsky and Wagner find places in Volume Three, the Editor would merely ask, in the words of a famous contemporary, 'What would you do?'

A. L. B.

CONTENTS

BEETHOVEN

BORN 16 December 1770   DIED 26 March 1827

By Peter Latham

Bonn (1770–1800)

Ludwig van Beethoven was born at Bonn on the Rhine. His father, Johann van Beethoven, had married in 1767 Maria Magdalena Laym, daughter of the head cook at the palace of Ehrenbreitstein. Their first child had died in infancy. Ludwig was the second. Of several others that followed, only two lived to grow up, Caspar Anton Karl, born in 1774, and Nicholas Johann, born in 1776. The family was of Flemish origin; it was Ludwig's grandfather who had established the branch in Bonn.

In those days Bonn derived most of its importance from being the seat of Maximilian Friedrich, Archbishop-Elector of Cologne; and Johann van Beethoven earned his living as a singer in the Electoral chapel. Johann was an easy-going man of weak character and he was anything but an ideal parent, for he was intemperate, this weakness becoming more marked as he got older. Nevertheless, it was he who first discovered Ludwig's unusual gifts, and with the memory of the young Mozart's triumphs fresh in his mind he hoped that his son might likewise win wealth and fame as a child prodigy. But the boy's genius was not of the kind that flowers prematurely, and when his disappointed father tried to drive him, he was met (we may guess) with a touch of Ludwig's characteristic obstinacy. And so we get our first glimpse of him as a tiny boy standing forlornly on a foot-stool in front of the keyboard, the tears streaming from his eyes.

With his music-teachers during his early years we need not concern ourselves. They had little influence on his future development. One of them, a certain Tobias Pfeiffer, was a boon companion of Johann van Beethoven's. We hear of them returning late from the wine-shop in a state of exaltation, rousing the little Ludwig from his bed and keeping him at the keyboard till dawn.

If he spent many such nights, it is no wonder that he appeared unusually quiet in the morning. He was sent to an elementary school, and there he is described as 'a shy and taciturn boy, observing more and pondering more than he spoke.' We also hear without surprise that he was unkempt and untidy. He learnt to read and to write a very fair hand (though in later life his letters grew more and more illegible). He picked up enough French to write intelligibly though atrociously in that language, and enough Latin to understand the texts he set. Spelling, even in his native German, was always shaky, and punctuation more shaky still: the mature Beethoven seldom ventured on anything more decisive than a comma. Arithmetic was beyond him. He might manage a little simple addition with the help of his ten fingers, but the calculations involved in financial transactions always gave him difficulty, and right at the end of his life the composer of the Ninth Symphony was being instructed by his nephew in simple multiplication—on his death-bed!

One must bear in mind that after the age of eleven he had no regular schooling except in music. Yet it is curious that an intellect so powerful in other directions should have failed so conspicuously in these elementary matters. One can only regard it as an example of Beethoven's general inability to adjust himself to the world around him. His intense absorption in the rich spiritual and artistic world he created prevented him from ever coming to terms with the life lived by ordinary mortals. This characteristic remained with him to the end and showed itself in other fields besides the intellectual. Physically he was clumsy: 'In his behaviour,' says Ries, who knew him well, 'Beethoven was awkward and helpless; his uncouth movements were often destitute of grace. He seldom took anything into his hands without dropping and breaking it. No piece of furniture was safe from him. He frequently knocked his ink-pot into the pianoforte. He could never learn to dance in time.' Socially he could never 'fit in.' He seemed incapable of realising that other people might quite honestly hold views different from his own, and he was prone to attribute base motives even to his closest friends whenever he found himself crossed. This curious limitation was generally at the root of the violent quarrels in which he so often involved himself; with his deafness, it helps to account for the unworthy suspicion with which he regarded almost everyone in his later years. In the whole of history there are few things more pathetic than the spectacle of the old lion, his brows wreathed with triumphant laurels and his sad eyes gazing out perplexedly on a world that so inexplicably failed to conform to his own fantastic conception of it.

In 1784 he secured the position of Assistant Organist in the Electoral chapel*—a proof that in his musical studies he had lacked neither diligence nor ability. Even before this date he had been taking some of the organist's work in an unofficial sort of way, and by this means he had come into touch with Christian Gottlob Neefe, the Court Organist at Bonn since 1782. Neefe seems to have understood the boy and appreciated his gifts. In addition to his duties at the organ, Ludwig was employed in the Court Theatre, occupying the important position of 'cembalist'. at the stage rehearsals (which involved reading from score at the keyboard).

* In this year the old Elector died and was succeeded by the Archduke Maximilian Franz, youngest son of the Empress Maria Theresa. But this did not affect the position of the Beethovens, father and son.

In the intervals of this excellent practical work Neefe put him through a fairly systematic course of composition. Later on, when he began to compose in earnest and was developing into a pianist of unusual ability, Neefe's good-will must have proved invaluable, especially in the matter of orchestral performances, and it was through Neefe again that the news of his youthful achievements became known in the larger musical world outside Bonn. When Ludwig migrated to Vienna he had still to learn counterpoint, but with this important exception he had been well grounded in composition, he had a few respectable works already to his credit, and he was a virtuoso pianist of outstanding merit and some fame. The credit for all this is largely due, as Beethoven himself acknowledged, to Neefe.

His first visit to Vienna was a brief one made in 1787, and is chiefly remarkable for his meeting with Mozart, then at the height of his fame. Mozart was not much impressed by his playing—he had doubtless heard better pianists than this youth of sixteen—but when Beethoven started to improvise, his attention was soon captured. Whether Beethoven actually took lessons from Mozart or not remains uncertain; but in any case he could not have had many. He arrived in Vienna about May; in early July he was hastening home—to his mother's death-bed.

Of his mother Beethoven always spoke with respect and affection. From her he must have received the love and the kindness that he sought in vain from his father. The little that is known of her suggests a prudent, rather dim woman, struggling gallantly but ineffectually in a sea of difficulties that at last overwhelmed her, and without the strength of will to exercise a decisive influence over her unruly family. She had always been delicate, and now the frail, tired body could struggle no longer. Ludwig arrived in time, and was with her when she died on 17th July.

He was left with a heavy load of care. His father's drunkenness was getting steadily worse and on one occasion he had to be rescued by his son from the police. Every year he grew less able to manage the family affairs and bit by bit his authority passed to Ludwig. His voice, too, began to show signs of wear, and in 1789 the Elector 'dispensed' with his services. Ludwig was eighteen, a tender age at which to assume the chief responsibility for such a household. But his duty was manifest and he undertook it without complaint. Fortunately he was now earning a rather larger salary.

It is a relief to turn from the dark picture of the Beethoven home and to find that Ludwig had good friends outside the family circle. Chief among these were the Breunings, to whom he ever afterwards referred as his 'guardian angels.' He began by making the acquaintance of Stephan von Breuning, a lad somewhat younger than himself, in whom he found a friend for life. Stephan had a younger brother, Lorenz, and a sister, Eleonora, and he persuaded his mother, who was a widow, to call in Beethoven to teach the pianoforte to both of them. Ludwig soon became intimate with the whole family and was constantly in and out of the house. The Breunings were well educated people, standing higher than the Beethovens in the social scale, and the influence of their culture was invaluable to the uncouth boy. With them he was happy. Frau von Breuning was one of the very few people who could manage him, and she did something to fill the ragged gap left by his mother's death. Lorenz died young. Eleonora was perhaps the only woman of approximately his own age for whom he entertained a deep affection quite untinged with sentimentality. In 1802 she married Doctor Wegeler, but this only served to draw Wegeler into the circle and made no difference to his wife's relations with Beethoven.

Another friend of these Bonn years was Ferdinand Ernst Gabriel, Count Waldstein. He arrived in Bonn in 1787 from the family seat at Dux,* and soon made the acquaintance of the young musician. Waldstein was a rich nobleman, a few years senior to Beethoven. Dr. Wegeler, Eleonora's husband, calls him a 'connoisseur and practitioner of music,' and says, 'We owe to this Mæcenas Beethoven's later fame.' Waldstein was well aware of Beethoven's poverty, and helped him from time to time with gifts of money, which he described on each occasion as 'a small gratuity from the Elector,' for fear of hurting his easily wounded pride. When, in November, 1792, Beethoven set out once again for Vienna, turning his back for ever, as it proved, on the city of his birth, he carried an encouraging letter in his pocket. It ran:

'DEAR BEETHOVEN! You are going to Vienna in fulfilment of your long-frustrated wishes. The genius of Mozart is mourning and weeping over the death of her pupil. She found a refuge but no occupation with the inexhaustible Haydn; through him she wishes to form a union with another. With the help of assiduous labour you shall receive Mozart's spirit from Haydn's hands.

'Your true friend,
'WALDSTEIN.'

A man of discernment, Count Waldstein!

The Virtuoso (1792–1800)

Apart from the project of taking lessons in counterpoint from Haydn, to which Count Waldstein alludes in his letter, it is very unlikely that Beethoven had any fixed plans when he reached Vienna towards the end of 1792. A young man

---

* The household of Dux included at this time a remarkable librarian, brought there in 1785 by Count Ferdinand's elder brother. Count Ferdinand, who spent much of his time at Dux, must have met him often; but we do not hear that he spoke of him to Beethoven. Beethoven, who censured Mozart's *Don Giovanni* for the coarseness of its libretto, would hardly have approved of—Casanova!

not quite twenty-two, he had come to the most musical city of Europe, the chosen home of Mozart and Haydn, to test himself by the severe standards he would find there. His future course must depend on the result of that test. Meanwhile, there was the counterpoint.

Haydn knew something of him. The old man had passed through Bonn in 1790 and, quite apart from that, he could hardly be ignorant of Beethoven's growing reputation as a pianist. The lessons began almost at once and continued for about a year. They were not a great success. Kind, easy-going 'Papa' Haydn hardly knew what to make of this outlandish youth from the provinces with his bad manners and boorish ways, who would never take any rule on trust, but must always know the 'why' as well as the 'how.' Beethoven on his side felt that he was getting nowhere and attributed his slow progress to Haydn's preoccupation with matters outside the lessons, and it certainly appears that the master, with many diverse calls upon his time, was sometimes a little careless in correcting his pupil's exercises. At the root of their failure to appreciate one another was a profound temperamental divergence, and it was perhaps a consciousness of this that made Beethoven refuse to describe himself as a pupil of Haydn in the dedication of the pianoforte sonatas, Op. 2. Yet they never quarrelled. Haydn watched the young man go his own tempestuous way, witnessed his triumphant progress as a virtuoso, gently reproved his overbearing manners by nicknaming him the 'Great Mogul,' but forbore to break with him, although there was much in Beethoven's music, even his early music, with which he could not sympathise. As to Beethoven, with all his ignorance of the world, he realised the value of Haydn's good-will and was careful not to offend him. For his counterpoint he went to Johann Schenk and then to Albrechtsberger, the strictest teacher of them all. The story that when working with Albrechtsberger he filled the margins of his exercises with sarcastic remarks is pure fiction.

Everything goes to show that from these lessons he got exactly what he wanted. Not even Albrechtsberger could make him a smooth and impeccable contrapuntist; but he took him as far as double fugue and triple counterpoint and he gave to his musical thought a contrapuntal turn, the healthy influence of which is everywhere apparent in the works composed after the conclusion of the lessons in 1795.

But the essential business of consolidating his technique and thus preparing the way for his future triumphs occupied only a small part of the young Beethoven's time and energies. Outside his study lay the whole city of Vienna with its manifold activities, and into these he threw himself heart and soul.

Vienna's reputation as a musical centre was due, first and foremost, to the enlightened patronage of the Austrian nobility. Many of them were connoisseurs of the art, nearly all of them enthusiasts. A few, like Prince Esterhazy, Haydn's old patron, could afford a private orchestra. For the less wealthy this was out of the question, but even they could hire a string quartet now and again or, failing that, a pianist. As a consequence there was an enormous demand for chamber music and instrumental players. Other branches of the art were comparatively neglected: there was an opera, but it was Italian; church music, Thayer tells us, was 'at a very low point' in 1793; and a public concert was a rarity.

With the Viennese aristocracy Beethoven's success was immediate and overwhelming. He had introductions from Count Waldstein, and it probably went for something that he came from the Elector at Bonn who was the Emperor's uncle, and that he was a pupil of the great Haydn. His music and his personality did the rest, and he soon made a reputation for himself both as pianist and teacher. He was in constant demand at the houses of the rich and for several years he had rooms of his own at Prince Carl Lichnowsky's. A glance at the dedications of the first half of the piano sonatas gives one an idea of the class of people he mixed with. There is no need here to copy that list of sonorous titles.

Beethoven refused from the first to adopt the subservient attitude that the patrons of music had been wont to expect from its practitioners. He would meet them as an equal or not at all. Even on that footing he was not an easy guest to entertain. Arrogant, sensitive, afraid of ridicule, and quite unable to hold his own in a battle of words, he often flew into a passion on the most trifling provocation and rewarded the kindness of his hosts with the grossest rudeness. The conditions of his early life had made him uncontrolled, emotional, self-willed, and with the coming of success the flaws in his character became apparent. We must distinguish carefully between character and personality. Even in these early years no one could fail to be impressed with the force of Beethoven's personality. But his character lacked firmness. Unlike those ancient worthies whose stoical constancy he so much admired in Plutarch's account of them, he was easily puffed up by good-fortune and as easily cast down by failure. Just now his star was in the ascendant and he was becoming more and more conscious of unusual power within him, with the result that his head was turned and his manners suffered.

Yet the Viennese aristocracy would never have tolerated him had they not discerned qualities that more than counterbalanced his insolence and conceit. His genius, his magnetic personality were acknowledged by all, and there was besides a gaiety and animation about the young Beethoven that people found immensely attractive. The troubles of his boyhood were behind him: his father had died very shortly after his departure from Bonn, and by 1795 both his brothers were established in Vienna, Caspar Karl as a musician, Johann as an apothecary. During his first few months in the capital he had indeed been desperately poor, depending as he did very largely on the small salary allowed him by the Elector. But all that was over now. He had no responsibilities and his music was bringing in enough to keep him in something like affluence. He had a servant, for a short time he even had a horse; he bought smart clothes, he learnt to dance (though not with much success), and there is mention of his wearing a wig! We must not allow our picture of the later Beethoven to throw its dark colours over these years of his early triumphs. He was a young giant exulting in his strength and his success, and youthful confidence gave him a buoyancy that was both attractive and infectious. Even in 1791, before he left Bonn, Carl Junker could describe him as 'this amiable, light-hearted man.' And in Vienna he had much to raise his spirits and nothing (at first) to depress them.

Within a comparatively short time after his arrival Beethoven had become, after Haydn, the most eminent musician in the city. As a pianist he took Vienna by storm. More finished, more elegant playing his audience had perhaps heard, but never such power, such fire, above all, such improvising. He made his first appearances before a public audience at two charity concerts in March, 1795, and the very fact of his engagement on these important occasions bears witness to his growing reputation. Soon he was the unquestioned king of Viennese pianists—'the giant among pianoforte players,' one admirer calls him. Whenever a travelling virtuoso visited the city it was with Beethoven that he was inevitably compared, and in this way he had to measure himself against the greatest masters in Europe. Joseph Wölffl was in Vienna in 1798, J. B. Cramer a year or two later: if Beethoven could maintain his supremacy against such competition as theirs he must indeed have been a remarkable pianist. It is pleasant to record that he established excellent relations with both Wölffl and Cramer; in spite of his 'somewhat haughty pose' he could respect and appreciate a great rival. His pupils included such notable performers as Ferdinand Ries and Carl Czerny, besides a number of young ladies of title, many of whom played excellently.

He himself made more than one concert tour during the

period under consideration. Prague was visited twice, Berlin once, and possibly Dresden, Nuremberg and other places. At times he thought of leaving Vienna permanently, of moving to Paris, perhaps, or London. But his characteristic irresolution kept him from any decisive step, and in the end Vienna held him. Every summer, however, he would pay a long visit to the country, taking rooms in Mödling, Heiligenstadt, Teplitz, or some other pleasant resort, or staying with his friends the Brunswicks in Hungary or the Lichnowskys in Silesia. There he would take long walks, for he loved the country passionately and drew from the beautiful works of nature his clearest intimations of the divine Artist. This habit of walking, so good for body and mind alike, remained with him through life. In his pocket he would carry the inevitable scrap of music paper on which to jot down any ideas that came to him, and often he would ensconce himself in the fork of a tree or some other convenient resting-place to consider, or even to work out on paper, the great lines of some new masterpiece.

In 1800 Beethoven brought out his eleventh piano sonata (in B flat, Op. 22). His works at that time included the piano trios, Op. 1, the string trios, Op. 9, the 'cello sonatas, Op. 5, and the violin sonatas, Op. 12. He had written two piano concertos and the third (in C minor, Op. 37) appeared in 1800, as did also the septet, Op. 20, the first six string quartets, Op. 18, and the first symphony, Op. 21. Most of these, it will be noticed, are chamber compositions, and their dedications generally indicate the patron for whom they were written. A dedication by Beethoven was usually a matter of business. Some rich nobleman would commission a work from him and pay for it. In return for this he would receive the manuscript with a dedication and have the exclusive use of it for an agreed period—six months, as a rule. After that the autograph reverted to Beethoven, who was then free to make his own arrangements concerning publication. There were exceptions, of course: Beethoven was very angry when his lifelong friend, Nicolaus Zmeskall, tried to give him a present in return for the dedication of the F minor quartet, Op. 95. But these disinterested dedications are rare, and we must be on our guard against reading any romantic significance into his numerous dedications to ladies with charming names and impressive titles. They were generally in return for cash down.

On the other hand we have abundant testimony that Beethoven was constantly in love. Indeed he was seldom out of it. Already in Bonn he had afforded more than one instance of his susceptibility, and in Vienna the list of ladies he had loved and lost soon grew really imposing. Few women could hold him for long; on one occasion he laughingly boasted of his constancy because he had worshipped at the shrine of the same divinity for the unprecedented period of seven months. How many of these episodes were serious, how many mere diversions, it is impossible to say. He proposed marriage to Magdalena Willmann in 1794, and probably to Therese Malfatti in 1810; and very likely he entertained serious thoughts of matrimony with two other ladies, the Countess Giulietta Guicciardi and the Countess Therese von Brunswick. Undoubtedly he longed to get married, to settle his vagabond life on a regular basis and to have children; a sidelight is thrown on his conception of the married state by his refusal ever to flirt with a married woman. Yet he never found a wife. It was not that he was unattractive to women; though clumsy and by no means handsome,* he was continually surprising his friends

* Beethoven was not more than five feet five inches in height, but his frame was muscular and well-knit, and the splendid head was set on magnificent shoulders. Like many of his contemporaries he was pock-marked, the result of an attack of small-pox in his childhood. The grim line of the mouth, which contributes so much to the tragic effect of the later portraits, was not nearly so noticeable in his early years, when his expression was much more animated.

by the difficult and unexpected conquests he made. Many of these ladies were far above him in station, and the difference in rank, combined with his reputation for eccentricity, must often have imposed an insurmountable barrier against matrimony. But equally often, one is inclined to think, the obstacle lay in himself: he idealised women, idealised them romantically without any reference to realities; and one after another the girls on whom he cast his eyes were discarded because they failed to live up to his impossible standards.

He remained celibate; but in spite of his high-mindedness he was not quite untouched by the moral laxity of his times. Thayer makes the unqualified assertion that he was not chaste; and although he suppresses the evidence, Thayer was far too conscientious a biographer to make a positive statement of that kind without being sure of his facts. Did Beethoven in these years of early manhood commit some foolish indiscretion for which he had to pay a terrible penalty? There is strong reason to believe he did, though in my opinion the case is not conclusively proved. If indeed it were, it would not only account for his celibacy, but provide us at last with a plausible theory of the appalling calamity that was so soon to darken his horizon and turn the story of his life to tragedy.

The Master (1800–1812)

Up to the year 1800 Beethoven's Viennese public regarded him first and foremost as a virtuoso of the pianoforte. Of course he was a composer as well—most pianists composed in those days—and there was a boldness and originality about his works which made them unusually interesting. But had he died in 1800, it is as a pianist that they would have mourned him. By the end of the next decade all this was altered: as a pianist he had ceased to count, but he had become incomparably the greatest composer of his day. The change in his orientation was the result of a catastrophe. Beethoven lost his hearing.

He himself indicates 1798 as the year in which he first noticed signs of this dreadful affliction. He did not take it very seriously to begin with. He had been suffering a good deal from a kind of dysentery and he thought the weakness in his ears was very likely associated with the weakness in his stomach. It would soon pass! But instead of passing it became worse, till in 1800 Thayer describes it as a 'chronic and increasing evil.' By this time Beethoven was really anxious. He did not yet anticipate that he would become completely deaf, but he was already wondering whether his ears would ever regain their original acuteness. He abandoned his plans of travel, took medical advice and tried various treatments. His friends had not yet noticed his misfortune, and for the present he keeps his secret jealously guarded. If they are struck by anything unusual they will attribute it, he knows, to his absent-mindedness. This policy of concealment was suggested in part by his natural sensitiveness, but in part also by fears for his professional prospects. What hope was there for a musician who was deaf? And it succeeded so well that even his pupil, Ferdinand Ries, who was with him constantly, dates his malady from 1802. Earlier than that he has noticed nothing.

But the doctors could do little to check the steady onward march of his complaint, and in 1801 his distress is such that he can keep silence no longer. In two poignant letters of June that year,* one to his dear friend, Karl Amenda, the other to Dr. Wegeler, he opens his heart, lays bare his misery and begs for sympathy and advice. In the fullness of his pride and strength the young genius has been struck down by an enemy against whom neither pride nor strength

---

* Or just possibly of June 1800: in this instance, as in many others, we cannot be quite sure when the letters were written.

avails him. He had looked forward to a brilliant and glorious career. Now he sees in front of him—nothing! 'My hearing has grown steadily worse for three years,' he writes to Wegeler. 'My ears whistle and buzz continually night and day. Heaven knows what will become of me!' He withdraws from society, avoids the brilliant gatherings wherein he had been wont to shine, because he cannot bring himself to the confession 'I am deaf!'

But now came a short idyll to bring temporary relief. On 16th November, in another letter to Wegeler, he says that he is being coaxed out of his retirement 'by a dear, fascinating girl who loves me and whom I love.' This was the Countess Giulietta Guicciardi, a near relation of his friends the Brunswicks, and to her he dedicated the sonata in C sharp minor, Op. 27, No. 2, the work that will probably always be known as the 'Moonlight Sonata.'* He was certainly in love with her for a while and probably she with him, though, as usual with Beethoven, the affair came to nothing. The romantic qualities of the sonata have induced some writers to regard it almost as an autobiographical document. Actually, the work that Beethoven originally sent to the Countess was the Rondo in G, Op. 51, No. 2, a graceful but not particularly significant piece. Desiring later to represent the Rondo to someone else, he recalled it and gave Giulietta the sonata in its place. Its origin, so far as it had an origin outside the world of tone, is probably to be found in a poem by Seume, *Die Beterin.* In 1803 the Countess Giulietta Guicciardi married Count Gallenberg, but by that time Beethoven was busy with the 'Eroica.'

---

* Beethoven never gave it this title; nor did he call the F minor 'Appassionata.' He is responsible for the title 'Les Adieux, l'Absence et le Retour,' of the sonata in E flat, Op. 81A, and he at least acquiesced in calling the early C minor, Op. 13, 'Sonata Pathétique.' All the other fancy names for sonatas were given without his sanction.

We may therefore reject the romantic legend that makes of Giulietta the supreme, unique love of Beethoven's life. Yet there is reason to believe that the impression she made on him was no light one. A medallion portrait of her was found among his effects after his death, and in a secret drawer of his desk was a letter, the most passionate love-letter Beethoven ever wrote. But there are difficulties about this letter. In dating it Beethoven has omitted the year, and though he gives the day of the week and the day of the month we have cause to suspect that either or both these dates may be wrong—he was notoriously careless about such things. We do not know from where it was sent—there is no address—nor even whether it was actually sent at all. And lastly no name is mentioned: the object of his adoration is called only the 'Immortal Beloved.' The weight of opinion inclines to Giulietta as the recipient of this mysterious letter; but Thayer votes for Therese von Bruns-wick, and Magdalena Willmann, Therese Malfatti and Amalie Sebald has each her champion. A truly singular uncertainty!

By 1802 most of Beethoven's intimates were aware of his deafness, but as he still withheld his confidence they dared not show their sympathy. His love affair was over now and he was left more and more alone to brood. That summer he went to Heiligenstadt, and there things reached a climax. In deep seclusion, remote from his friends, he fought his battle, and the echoes of it only come down to us through that strange document known as the Heiligenstadt Will. He never seriously contemplated suicide, but he does seem at this period to have anticipated an early death, and so he writes the 'Will' and addresses it to his two brothers. Testamentary disposition occupy but a small part; the bulk of it is concerned with an account of his illness, laments over his lot, invocations to himself to be patient, to endure (since nothing else now remains), and an exhortation to his brothers that they train their children in virtue. The whole document is too long to transcribe, but the postscript with its passionate cry of despair may be quoted:

'Heiligenstadt, October 10th, 1802, thus do I take my farewell of thee—and indeed sadly—yes, that beloved hope—which I brought with me when I came here to be cured at least in a degree—I must wholly abandon, as the leaves of Autumn fall and are withered so hope has been blighted, almost as I came—I go away—even the high courage—which often inspired me in the beautiful days of summer—has disappeared—O Providence—grant me at last but one day of pure *joy*—it is so long since real joy echoed in my heart—O when—O when, O Divine One—shall I feel it again in the temple of nature or of men—Never? no—O that would be too hard.'

This is the very climax of his agony. At the internal struggles which followed we can only guess, but we know that he emerged victorious. To suffering, to renunciation, he resigned himself since he must. But he could still compose and in his compositions he would triumph! How magnificently he rose to his destiny is shown by the works that followed. From Heiligenstadt he returned with the sunny second symphony, the most light-hearted of them all!—a warning to those who insist on reading a composer's life into his work. In 1803 he embarked on an even vaster project, the 'Eroica.' This was finished in 1804, and during that year and the next he was busy with his opera, 'Fidelio.' In 1806 comes the fourth symphony, in 1807 the fifth (which was actually begun before the fourth). 1808 brought the 'Pastoral,' 1812 the seventh and eighth symphonies. Was there ever such a flood of masterpieces? And our list takes no account of the Mass in C, the two last pianoforte concertos, the violin concerto, the 'Coriolan' and 'Egmont' overtures, the Rasoumovsky quartets, and a whole sheaf of sonatas, including the most famous of all, for piano solo or for piano and violin—though all these works and others besides belong to the same overwhelming period. Yet all the while the

composer was growing deafer and deafer, till in 1810 Bettina
Brentano had to write her share of her conversations with
him on paper.

The piano he continued to play as long as he could. Early
in this epoch Czerny could still speak of him as a virtuoso
and say, 'Nobody equalled him in the rapidity of his scales,
double trills, skips, etc.—not even Hummel.' Even much
later, in 1811, when Czerny took piano lessons from him,
he found that he still 'corrected with the greatest exactitude.'
But by that time he had ceased to be a soloist. His last public
appearance as a virtuoso was in 1808, though he still continued to play in chamber music and his improvisations
remained impressive till a much later date. Conducting too
he found quite practicable, and most of the masterpieces of
the period were performed for the first time under his
direction.

As his malady got worse Beethoven abandoned his pathetic
efforts to conceal it. Among the sketches for the Rasoumovsky quartets he writes: 'Let your deafness no longer
remain a secret—not even in art!' He mingled once again
in society, laughed, flirted as before. Life had played him
a sorry trick, but he would triumph in spite of it—he would
even be happy! Thanks to the success of his work he was
comfortably off, and as he sat talking and jesting with his
friends he was often cheerful, even gay—although by 1804
it was already becoming an effort to converse with him.
Yet the crisis had left its mark, and in the same year (1804)
Stephan von Breuning, writing to Wegeler, speaks of the
'indescribable, I might say fearful effect of the gradual loss
of hearing,' and mentions 'reserve, mistrust' among the
qualities that he now observes in his old friend. The deaf
often become mistrustful and Beethoven's keen sensibilities
combined with his loss of hearing to produce what may
almost be called suspicion-mania. He suspected his household, his business associates, even his friends, in the most
unwarrantable way and thereby added much to his own

sufferings. Accounts of quarrels grow more frequent, and he is continually changing his servants or his lodgings.

It will have been noticed that the portion of Beethoven's life we are now considering coincided roughly with the great victories of Napoleon Bonaparte. Beethoven always regarded himself as a democrat, though his opinions were never of the violent kind, and they matured eventually into a steady if rather unexpected admiration of the English people and their constitution. The startling rise of Napoleon he watched with deep interest. To him the great Corsican appeared as the champion of an ideal Freedom, and it was in his honour that the 'Eroica' symphony was composed. Early in the spring of 1804 the score was ready for dispatch to Paris, with Napoleon's name on the title-page, when the news arrived that the First Consul had proclaimed himself Emperor. In an access of rage and disappointment that his hero should prove so false to his conception of him, Beethoven tore out his dedication and substituted a new one, to Prince Lobkowitz. Some years later, in 1809, the artillery of Napoleon was battering at the gates of Vienna—and the composer lay in a cellar, his head smothered in pillows, desperately endeavouring to preserve the poor remnants of his hearing from the shattering effects of the bombardment.

Another light is thrown on Beethoven's democratic principles by an incident that occurred during the few days that he spent in the company of the poet Goethe. It was in Teplitz during the summer of 1812. Not long before Beethoven had written his music to Goethe's 'Egmont,' and Goethe's interest in Beethoven had been aroused by the enthusiastic accounts he had received from their mutual friend, Bettina Brentano. For a week or so in June they saw a good deal of each other. They went for walks together, and on one occasion, Bettina tells us, they met the Empress and the whole Court. Goethe stood aside, bowing obsequiously. Beethoven made straight through the throng, merely acknowledging to right and left the greetings of his acquaintances. The difference between democratic independence and mere bad manners was not, apparently, very clear to him.

PER ARDUA AD ASTRA (1812–27)

> '*Speak of me as I am; nothing extenuate,*
> *Nor set down aught in malice : then, must you speak*
> *Of one that lov'd, not wisely, but too well;*
> *Of one not easily jealous, but, being wrought,*
> *Perplex'd in the extreme.*'

After the sustained creative energy of the years 1800 to 1812, Beethoven's genius slept, or at least dozed, so far as published works are concerned, for a number of years. A pair of piano sonatas, another pair for 'cello, an overture (not one of the best) and a song-cycle, are the pick of his works in these lean years. But in 1817 the flame bursts out again and he sets to work simultaneously on three of his mightiest undertakings, the piano sonata in B flat, Op. 106, the Mass in D, and the ninth symphony, which occupy him between them till 1824, the three last piano sonatas being thrown off during intervals of work on the two gigantic choral masterpieces. Then he turns to quartets, producing his last five compositions in this *genre* between 1824 and the onset of his illness in 1826. The quartets were by no means intended as his final word. There are sketches for a new symphony and a string quintet in C, and he often spoke of another Mass, a second opera, possibly a *Faust* to crown his life's achievement. But these things were not to be.

For most serious musicians these last works are the greatest of all. It is not merely their size that gives us this impression, though in fact they are his biggest; nor is it their novelty, though in them Beethoven innovates more boldly than ever before. It is not even their wealth of ideas, though the last quartets are perhaps more closely packed with thought than any other music in the world. It has been said that there is a spiritual, mystical quality about them, but the same is true of many compositions by Palestrina, Bach, and others. What is unique about this music is not its spirituality, but its particular *kind* of spirituality, the note of authentic experience, the peace that is only won through strife, the wisdom that only suffering can teach.* There is no sudden crisis to account for this final development of Beethoven's style; it was the result of a gradual process that included the whole man and proceeded uninterrupted to the end. The last quartets take us a step further than the ninth symphony. Had Beethoven lived to write yet other works, it is safe to surmise that they would have taken us further still.

The sketch-books in which Beethoven worked out his ideas afford evidence of his mental process at this time. Many are still extant and have been made the subjects of most careful study. Nottebohm is our chief authority here, and one of the things that strikes him most is the profuseness of invention. No one, he says, who has not seen the sketch-books can appreciate the full measure of Beethoven's fertility. The published works, rich though they be, contain but a tithe of what the composer might have produced.

Even during the barren years, 1813–17, his inspiration was still flowing, and the scarcity of works must be attributed in part to sheer lack of resolution. His character always lacked decision and his infirmity of will grew on him as he got older. It was this that kept him from going to England. He had always admired the English, he wanted to visit London, and during his later years he received more than one invitation. He was assured that such an expedition would be highly remunerative, and once, at any rate, he almost made up his mind to go. Almost!—and then that fatal irresolution came over him and he jettisoned his plans. It was the same with composition on the large scale: his projects had become so vast that he simply could not bring

* On this subject see J. W. N. Sullivan's *Beethoven: His Spiritual Development.*

himself to embark upon them. It must be admitted that he had cause for hesitation, for when, in 1817, he took the plunge and started work on the Mass and the ninth symphony, he thereby committed himself to some six years of arduous labour. His artistic conscience was more sensitive than ever, his critical faculty keener. What might have been good enough ten years earlier was not nearly good enough now. He wrote and rewrote with astonishing assiduity and patience; the contrapuntal sections in the Mass were only hammered out by sheer tenacity and indomitable perseverance; he would wrestle with them for hours and then come from his study exhausted as if by actual physical conflict. Even when the score was finished he was loth to part with it, keeping it by him day after day, week after week, in the hope that some improvement might suggest itself.

Unhappily this extreme scrupulousness, so conspicuous in matters connected with his art, was by no means so evident at this time in his dealings with his fellow men. One records with regret that the ninth symphony, after being definitely commissioned by the London Philharmonic Society, received its first performance in Vienna* and was dedicated to the King of Prussia; and that the Mass, after being promised to three rival publishers simultaneously, was ultimately given to a fourth. Throughout these dubious negotiations Beethoven was loud in his protestations of his own uprightness, and it may be that, with his curious incapacity to adjust himself to the external world, he was blind to the discreditable nature of his transactions. But while we may seek to understand his attitude we cannot condone his conduct. If Beethoven really regarded as honourable his proceedings in the matter of the Mass, then one can only lament the flaw in his moral sense. One might even suspect him of avarice, were it not that in his

* On 7th May, 1824.

later years he was badly in need of money. This was due in part to his own improvidence, in part to the unfruitful years that preceded 1818; but there were more serious causes, and these we must now investigate.

In 1812 Beethoven's financial position seemed secure. He was drawing a considerable income from his compositions and in addition he was in receipt of an annuity of four thousand florins that had been settled on him in 1809 by three rich patrons, the Archduke Rudolph (youngest son of the Emperor Leópold the second), Prince Kinsky, and Prince Lobkowitz. Through no fault of its generous guarantors this annuity became a source of endless worry to Beethoven. First there was a fall in the Austrian currency; then Prince Kinsky was killed in an accident and Prince Lobkowitz went bankrupt. Beethoven found himself involved with a swarm of lawyers, executors and creditors. In the end he got his annuity—or most of it. But the business dragged on till 1815, making serious inroads on his time and energy.

Meanwhile he had undertaken another lawsuit on his own account. Mälzel, the inventor of the metronome, had also invented a strange mechanical instrument which he called the Panharmonicon, and in 1813 he prevailed upon Beethoven to write a work for it. This composition, perhaps the worst, but in its day the most popular that ever came from Beethoven's pen, was the 'Battle Symphony: Wellington's Victory at Vittoria.' At Mälzel's suggestion he orchestrated it, and it was performed at a concert on 8th December, 1813, amid scenes of great enthusiasm. Afterwards, however, Mälzel and Beethoven fell out over their respective rights in the work, and Beethoven went to law. Mälzel fought the case and there were years of fruitless conflict before the litigants made peace. Beethoven gained nothing, and this time he had wasted money as well as energy.

Far more serious was the family lawsuit that raged round his nephew Karl. Both Beethoven's brothers had married, Caspar Karl in 1806, Johann in 1812. Johann had prospered and become, in his own eyes at any rate, a person of some consequence. Caspar Karl had been less successful and in 1815 he died, leaving a young son, Karl, who was placed under the joint guardianship of his mother and his uncle Ludwig.

His sisters-in-law Beethoven hated with a deep and bitter hatred. Since both ladies were shameless in their infidelities his feelings are comprehensible enough; but they did not help him in his position as guardian. His first action was to remove Karl entirely from his mother's influence, in direct opposition to the terms of the will, on the plea that she was not a fit person to have charge of him. The mother's resentment was natural, for whatever her faults she loved her son; and it is not in the least surprising that she sought redress at law.

She had more to complain of than the usurpation of her rights as a mother. In everything except his motives Beethoven was the most unsuitable of guardians. His habits were irregular, his lodgings untidy, uncomfortable, even dirty; and his frequent preoccupation prevented him from giving proper attention to the boy's material needs. Evidence was brought to show that Karl's feet and hands were frost-bitten, that he had no seasonable clothes, that his linen and his baths were neglected. On the moral side Beethoven was equally unwise, kind and harsh by turns. Never knowing what treatment to expect, Karl grew deceitful, lying freely to his uncle when there was danger of an outburst. He was not naturally a vicious boy and he became eventually a decent member of society, but it was inevitable that he should react unfavourably to the unhappy influences of such a childhood. He told the court that he 'would like to live with his uncle if he had but a companion, as his uncle was hard of hearing and he could not talk to him.'

As for Beethoven, he was entirely convinced of the justice of his own cause, and, as usual, he was completely unable to look at things from the point of view of other people. In Karl he had found at last an abiding object for his love, and this time he did not love by halves. The boy was all in all to him, and on him he lavished all the passionate affection of his lonely spirit. 'God help me,' he writes in one place, 'Thou seest me deserted by all men, for I do not wish to do wrong, hear my supplication, only for the future to be with my Karl.' For all his wrongheadedness the desperate sincerity of the man compels our sympathy. Towards him, as towards Karl and his mother, there is no room for any feeling but a profound pity. Providence granted his prayer: at last, in 1820, the court gave final judgment and Beethoven was confirmed in his guardianship of Karl. But his nephew's heart he could not win. Karl accepted the situation, though for his deaf old uncle with his queer temper and bearish ways it was fear and impatience, certainly not love, that he felt.

The lawsuit had been a heavy drain on Beethoven's resources, and Karl's education involved considerable further expense. He was poor now, for the first time since his early days in Vienna, and he was very much alone. It was about 1812 that he began to withdraw from society. His law cases occupied much of his time, there was his composition, and soon his nephew provided an all-absorbing interest at home. Besides, he was now too deaf to mingle easily with a crowd of people. In 1814 he took part in chamber music for the last time, and the next year made his final public appearance at the piano, playing accompaniments for the singer Wild.* By 1819 it was no longer possible to converse with him even by shouting. 'Fidelio' was revived in November, 1822, and it was at a rehearsal for this performance that he had to abandon conducting. In spite of the utmost good-will on the part of all concerned it soon

* The audience at this concert was full of notabilities (including crowned heads) assembled for the Congress of Vienna.

B

became impossible to go on. Beethoven looked round, hesitating, anxious. Then realisation came to him. 'He leaped from his place in the orchestra, hastened from the theatre to his lodgings, threw himself on the sofa, covered his face with his hands.'* It was the end. At the first performance of the ninth symphony in 1824 he stood in the orchestra near the singers and was quite unaware of the storm of applause till Fräulein Unger drew his attention to the clapping hands he could see but not hear.

He gradually became something of a recluse, and people who had come to Vienna on purpose to see him were sometimes unable to discover whether he was in the city or not. His poverty never amounted to destitution, but he was hard pressed, and his pathetic inability to govern his household with order and economy added greatly to his difficulties. There was indeed a nest-egg (amounting to over seven thousand florins) on which he might have drawn, but this had been put aside as his legacy to Karl, and whatever his need he refused to touch it. We hear of threadbare coats and soiled linen. Once, out walking in the country he was arrested as a tramp, and his protests that he was the composer Beethoven were met with amused incredulity. Not such, in the opinion of the police, would the great Beethoven appear. Ill-health was added to his other woes: he had trouble with his eyes, he suffered from various ailments that kept him for a while in bed, and in 1821 he was laid up with a serious attack of jaundice.

Neither poverty, loneliness nor suffering could make him understand the world and its unaccountable human inhabitants. Yet few men had been purged like Beethoven, and the white flame of the chastened spirit was often visible through the mask of misery that was his face. Sir Julius Benedict describes him in 1823, his 'white hair flowing over his mighty shoulders [and] with that wonderful look.'

---

* The story is Schindler's, who was present.

Rellstab, in 1825, is more explicit: 'Suffering, melancholy and goodness showed in his face, but not a sign of harshness.' Beethoven had learnt something more than resignation, an ultimate wisdom the clue to which we must seek in the last quartets. Even then we shall probably seek in vain, for there are high mysteries here.

In 1826 his relations with his nephew reached a crisis. Karl, now a young man of university age, was lazy and neglectful of his uncle. Beethoven was suspicious and reproachful, always carping at him and accusing him of visiting his mother—the unforgivable sin! At last, exasperated and desperate, Karl tried to shoot himself; but the wound was not mortal and after a sojourn in hospital he recovered. The tragedy occurred at the end of July and the shock aged Beethoven visibly. It was now clear even to his vacillating mind that a decisive step was necessary, and on the advice of his family he resolved to gratify Karl's own wishes and send him into the army.

A vacancy was found, but there was an inevitable interval after Karl's discharge from hospital on 25th September before he could take up his cadetship. Johann van Beethoven stepped into the breach and invited uncle and nephew to stay with him on his estate at Gneixendorf. The visit was planned to last a fortnight. But the fortnight passed and Ludwig, his usual indecision reinforced by his dread of losing Karl, made no move to leave. Johann's wife returned to Vienna; Johann himself stayed on, behaving all the time with exemplary patience. When towards the end of November he pointed out to Ludwig that Karl's prospects in the army might be jeopardised if there was further delay, he was doing no more than his duty, and it is Ludwig's hasty temper that we must blame for what ensued. He took deep offence at his brother's well-meant intervention and insisted on leaving at once. Johann, after vainly urging him to postpone his departure till adequate arrangements could be made, did his best to secure a suitable vehicle at short notice and speed the travellers on their way. But the journey in the raw winter weather was inevitably uncomfortable, Beethoven had to spend the night in a draughty room at an inn, and when he arrived in Vienna on 2nd December he was already in a fever.

At first he made light of it, and it was only on the third day that Dr. Wawruch was called in. He found his patient suffering from pneumonia, prescribed the proper treatment and in a week had him on his legs again. But the next day he relapsed with alarming symptoms and it was soon clear that all sorts of complications had developed, including jaundice and dropsy. The real root of the trouble was cirrhosis of the liver. He had probably been suffering from this complaint for a long time; it may well have been the cause of his jaundice in 1821, and now it killed him.

Karl had to join his regiment at the beginning of the new year (1827). He departed and never saw his uncle again. But Beethoven's friends, Schindler, Breuning, his brother Johann, and several others were assiduous at his bedside. His illness did nothing to sweeten his temper, but at first he was in good heart in spite of the wretchedly insanitary conditions in which he lay. He read Scott and Ovid and was immensely pleased with an edition of Handel's works sent him by an English admirer. News of his illness spread and he received many gratifying evidences of the veneration in which he was held. But as time went on and, in spite of a change of doctors and several changes of treatment, he got no better, hope gradually sank. On 16th March the doctors declared him lost. He already knew it.

Yet he lingered on. They brought him news that one of his last quartets had been performed but had failed to please. 'It will please them some day,' he answered tranquilly. The London Philharmonic Society, hearing of his illness and his need, sent him a loan of a hundred pounds; and one of his last actions was to dictate a letter of thanks to 'the generous

Englishmen.' On 23rd March it was apparent that the end was near. He signed his will, and his friends, in some trepidation (for they doubted his orthodoxy), asked if they might send for a priest. He raised no objection, received the Last Sacraments and offered a courteous word of thanks. All was now accomplished, and turning to those present he exclaimed with a flicker of his old spirit, '*Plaudite, amici, comœdia finita est.*' Next day, the 24th, a present of good Rhine wine arrived from Schott's, his publishers. 'Pity, pity,' he murmured, 'too late!' They were his last words. That evening he relapsed into unconsciousness, but for hour after hour his iron constitution fought a last great fight with Death. He lived through the night, through the next day, and on the afternoon of the 26th he still breathed. That evening there was snow in Vienna, and an unexpected thunderstorm. A particularly violent thunderclap seemed to rouse Beethoven. He raised his clenched right hand with a 'very earnest' expression in his eyes. When it fell back he was dead.

They buried him with what honour they might. A huge crowd that included the élite of the Viennese aristocracy followed the coffin to the Währing cemetery, and there they laid him, putting above him a stone inscribed with the one word 'Beethoven.' Among the torch-bearers was Franz Schubert, whom Beethoven never knew but whose songs he had admired on his death-bed. Late in the following year Schubert was to travel that road again, to be laid near him. But neither Beethoven nor Schubert was left undisturbed. In 1888 the remains were exhumed, to be re-interred, let us hope finally, in the central cemetery of Vienna. Not far off lies Hugo Wolf.

BIBLIOGRAPHY

GRACE, HARVEY: *Beethoven*. 3s. 6d. (Curwen, 'Masters of Music' Series, 1927.)

NEWMAN, ERNEST: *The Unconscious Beethoven.* O.P. (Cassell, 1927.)

SHEDLOCK, J. S.: *Letters of Ludwig van Beethoven.* 2 vols. O.P. (Dent, 1909.)

SHEDLOCK, J. S.: *A Selection of Beethoven's Letters.* 10s. 6d. (Dent, 1926.)

SULLIVAN, J. W. N.: *Beethoven; his Spiritual Development.* 4s. 6d. (Cape, 'Life and Letters' Series, 1927.)

THAYER, A. W.: *The Life of Ludwig van Beethoven.* 3 vols. £5 5s. (Beethoven Association, New York, 1920.)

TURNER, W. J.: *Beethoven; the Search for Reality.* 6s. (Dent, 1927.)

LOUIS HECTOR BERLIOZ

BORN 11 December 1803   DIED 8 March 1869

By Edwin Evans

Origins and Early Years

If one draws a straight line on the map from Vienne, on
the Rhône below Lyons, to Grenoble, the old capital of the
Dauphiné, there will be found on it, towards the centre but
slightly nearer to the former city, a small country town
called La Côte St. André. It lies on the slope of the Banchet
hills, with splendid views across country. There dwelt, for
about four centuries before the composer was born, the
family of Berlioz, whose name may perhaps indicate that
it originally hailed from Savoy. Its members had attained
to some distinction in official and professional life. The
composer's father, Louis Joseph Berlioz (1776–1848), had
studied medicine at Montpellier, established himself as a
physician and been appointed medical officer of health.
His mother came from Meylan, a village three miles beyond
Grenoble in the direction of Savoy, and bore before her
marriage the name of Marmion, in which Berlioz took
increased pride after he had become acquainted with Walter
Scott's poem. The first child of the marriage, he was born
at La Côte, and baptized when five days old with the names
of Louis Hector. He had five brothers and sisters, two of
whom died in childhood. Of the others, Nancy (1806–50)
married a magistrate of Grenoble, and Adèle (1814–60) a
lawyer of Vienne. Prosper, the youngest, was born seventeen years after the composer. His death in Paris at the age
of nineteen was a sad blow to him.

The boy's father was an enlightened liberal-minded man whose wide culture embraced an amateur's knowledge of music. His mother had strict religious views, which included a narrow prejudice against music, probably because of its association with the stage, more conspicuous in France and Italy than in Germany or England. Heredity can thus have played but a small part in forming young Hector's predisposition. This asserted itself at his First Communion when, as he related in his Memoirs, 'a new world of love and feeling was revealed' to him in the fresh young voices raised in the eucharistic hymn. In after years he was to discover that the melody which had so affected him had been adapted from D'Alayrac's opera 'Nina,' but he was then happily unaware of its secular origin. Not long afterwards he discovered in the house an old flageolet from which he strove to coax the tune of 'Malbrouk' with such effect that, in self-defence, his father taught him the rudiments of music. At the age of ten he was sent to a local school, but did not stay there long, his father taking charge of his general education. This included the reading of the classics, and laid the foundation of that deep love of Virgil which was, many years afterwards, to bear fruit in 'Les Troyens.' In the library at home he also discovered Florian's *Estelle et Némorin*, which he devoured in secret, and which became one of his favourite books. With it is associated a strange love of his boyhood wherein is revealed that remarkable capacity for intense emotion that was to remain through life a salient characteristic. The children were accustomed to pay a yearly visit to their maternal relations at Meylan. Not far away was a villa at which a certain Madame Gautier spent the summer with her two nieces, of whom the elder, aged eighteen, was named Estelle. For her the twelve-year-old boy developed an extraordinary infatuation, which threatened to make him the laughing stock of the country-side, especially as he suffered all the pangs of an intense jealousy concerning her. To him it was so far from being a laughing matter that when he saw her again, many years after, a married woman with a family, his heart was still stirred and to the end, though he had forgotten the colour of her hair, he still remembered her eyes.

About the same time his father attempted to begin his instruction in anatomy, with a view to his following his own profession, but from the first the boy held the subject in aversion. His love of music had meanwhile increased, and his father tried to turn it to account by promising him as a reward for his anatomical studies a new flute, an instrument on which he had already acquired some prowess, but his efforts were fated to be in vain. On the other hand, Berlioz *père*, having taught his son what he knew of music, suggested to his neighbours that they should combine with him to bring a music teacher from Lyons. This led to the engagement of a violinist named Imbert, who was provided with twelve pupils. Under his guidance the young musician, then fourteen, made rapid progress with the aid of an old copy he had discovered of Rameau's *Harmony* in the simplified edition of d'Alembert, and subsequently of the more practical treatise of Catel. Imbert was succeeded by an Alsatian named Dorant, whose accomplishments included the guitar. Berlioz was thus able to record himself in his Memoirs, 'master of three potent and incomparable instruments, the flageolet, flute and guitar.' Before that he had begun to compose: a 'Potpourri Concertant' for flute, horn and strings, two quintets for flute and strings, and a number of songs, mostly settings of verses from Florian's idyll, very sad and in a minor key. He even aspired to appear in print, for in the spring of 1819 he wrote to two Paris publishers offering them his 'Potpourri.' All these works were destroyed before he had left for Paris, but memories of two of them survive. The melody in B minor introduced by the violins soon after the beginning of the Allegro in the overture of 'Les Francs Juges' hails from the second of the quintets, and the air for the violins at the opening of the Largo of the 'Symphonie Fantastique' was originally a setting of some lines of La Fontaine which expressed his anguish at leaving the places hallowed by the footsteps of his Estelle.

Medicine or Music?

In October, 1821, Hector Berlioz and his cousin Alphonse Robert arrived in Paris, where they were to study medicine. The latter remained faithful to his task and became a well-known Paris doctor. Berlioz was at first animated by a sense of duty to his father. Although his first experience of the dissecting-room produced such horror that he jumped from the window and ran home, he strove to overcome this disgust and assiduously attended lectures. But music proved too strong for him. He began to frequent the opera. First he heard Salieri's 'Les Danaïdes,' with the dance-music added by Spontini. The following week he heard Méhul's 'Stratonice' followed by Persuis's ballet of 'Nina' in which he recognised, played on the cor anglais, the tune borrowed from D'Alayrac's opera of the same name which had so impressed him in childhood. He also discovered that the library of the Conservatoire was open to the public and spent many hours immersed in the scores of Gluck when he should have been studying medical treatises. It was a performance of that composer's 'Iphigénie en Tauride' that decided him. He wrote to his father that music must henceforth be his profession. At the library he had become acquainted with a Conservatoire student named Gerono, a pupil of Lesueur, who offered to present him to his teacher. Berlioz agreed and took with him a cantata for bass and orchestra, 'Le Cheval Arabe,' and a three-part canon which Lesueur pronounced to be full of vitality—and of faults. He arranged for Gerono to 'coach' his friend until he was ready for more advanced teaching. Early in 1823 Lesueur pronounced him ripe and accepted him as a personal pupil.

Meanwhile Hector's correspondence with his father upon the subject had been slow in coming to a head because, the École de Medécine having twice been closed for political causes, Berlioz could give good reasons for non-attendance, and his allowance of one hundred and twenty francs per month had not been stopped. Perhaps also the father may have had illusions concerning the rapidity of possible advancement in the musical profession, and expected some result from his son's enthusiasm. No sooner had young Berlioz been accepted by Lesueur than he must needs write an opera on the subject of Florian's *Estelle*, adapted by his friend Gerono. He afterwards declared himself fortunate in that nobody ever heard a note of it. This was followed by a scene for bass with orchestra from Saurin's drama *Beverley, ou le Joueur*, known in England as *The Gamester*. Then Masson, conductor at the Church of St. Roch, invited him to write a Mass for Holy Innocents' Day, the choirboys' feast-day, 28th December, 1823. He did so. Inadequately performed, it was a complete failure. He presented himself as a candidate at the Conservatoire, and failed to pass. Although Lesueur wrote personally to his father, the latter stopped the allowance and recalled his son to La Côte, where he had a hard struggle to overcome the parental opposition. He was, however, to have another chance. The allowance was restored and he was permitted to attend the Conservatoire. Returning to Paris he wrote an Oratorio, 'Le Passage de la Mer Rouge.' But the failure of his Mass still troubled him. Augustin de Pons, an amateur whose acquaintance he had made at the Opéra, advanced him twelve hundred francs to defray the cost of a worthy performance which took place 10th July, 1825. It aroused much enthusiasm among his friends . . . and left him owing twelve hundred francs. He went to live in a garret, made his meals of dry bread with prunes or dates, and gave lessons until he had reduced the debt by one half. Then unfortunately de Pons, distressed at such privations or possibly in need of the balance, wrote to his father, with the result that he was paid, and the allowance was once more suspended. But Berlioz recruited pupils whom he taught singing, the flute and the guitar, and presently secured an engagement as chorister at the Théâtre des Nouveautés which was sufficient to enable one of such frugal tastes as his to keep the wolf from the door. He shared rooms with a compatriot, Antoine Charbonnel, whose father had succeeded Berlioz senior as mayor of La Côte, and somehow contrived to purchase a piano for one hundred and ten francs.

The 'Prix de Rome'

Meanwhile his studies at the Conservatoire were progressing under Lesueur and Reicha, to whom Cherubini had assigned him for counterpoint. He was also busily engaged in composition. To this period belong the 'heroic scena' called 'La Révolution Grecque' and the monologue and bacchanale 'La Mort d'Orphée' with which he competed unsuccessfully for the *Prix de Rome* in 1827. His friend Humbert Ferrand having provided him with a libretto, he began the composition of an opera, 'Les Francs Juges,' the overture of which he considered to be his first important orchestral work. It was followed soon afterwards by the 'Waverley' Overture. In 1828 he competed again and won the second prize with the lyrical scena 'Herminie et Tancrède.' At the same time he was already engaged upon the eight scenes from Goethe's *Faust* which, completed in 1829, were subsequently to form the nucleus of 'La Damnation de Faust.' The same year he competed again for the *Prix de Rome* with 'La Mort de Cléopâtre,' in which he excelled himself, but the most striking original passage in the whole work proved too much for the judges, who decided not to award any first prize that year. In 1830 he again competed, with 'Sardanapale,' but by now he had learned his lesson. He sent the work in without the final conflagration, and this time, at last, he was awarded the long-coveted *premier prix*. He had now lost all illusions concerning the artistic aspect of the competition, but had persisted in his candidature, in view of the importance attached to a *Prix de Rome*, not only by the French musical world, but more especially by his father.

There had now, moreover, been two performances of note. On St. Cecilia's Day, 22nd November, 1827, his Mass was performed at St. Eustache, on which occasion he made his first appearance as conductor. On 26th May, 1828, he gave a concert of his works at the Conservatoire. The programme consisted of the overtures to 'Waverley' and 'Les Francs Juges,' an aria, and a trio with chorus from the latter work, 'La Révolution Grecque' and the 'Resurrexit' from the Mass. Apart from the trio, in which the chorus missed its cue, the concert went well, and brought the composer fame as 'the Byron of music.' The two overtures and the 'Resurrexit' were heard again at the Conservatoire on 1st November, 1829, as well as a vocal sextet, 'Concert des Sylphes,' from the 'Faust' music. This was rather poorly executed by Conservatoire students, and missed fire, but the other works were more successful than ever. This concert actually showed a profit of 150 francs. The *Prix de Rome* was then not yet won, but Berlioz had 'arrived.'

Shakespeare, Harriet and 'Camille'

Two years earlier, however, events had taken place which were to have a profound effect both on Berlioz's life and on his music. The romantic movement was at its height and Shakespeare, previously known only to the curious, was beginning to be widely read on the Continent. French students knew him through the adaptations of Ducis. Thereupon, in the autumn of 1827, Charles Kemble brought to the Odéon an English company, which included Harriet Smithson. She was then twenty-seven years old, having been born at Ennis, Ireland, on 18th March, 1800. All literary Paris flocked to the theatre. Shakespeare became 'the rage.' Berlioz relates that he was struck as by lightning, not only by Shakespeare, but by Miss Smithson as Ophelia and Juliet. He raved. He was exalted. There are fantastic stories, probably exaggerated but not without foundation, concerning his behaviour at that time. He did not speak her language, could not even pronounce her name, but he was madly in love. His letters remaining unanswered, he poured out his passion in settings of Moore's 'Irish Melodies.' It was mainly to attract her attention that he gave that concert in May, 1828, and she did not even hear of it. Not until the eve of her departure for Holland did she learn of the musician's infatuation and then she declared that it was hopeless, but he was elated because at least she was aware of his existence. It was in this love-fever that he began the composition of the 'Symphonie Fantastique; Episode in the Life of an Artist,' in which the *idée fixe* represents his obsession. He heard some scandal concerning his idol—its nature has not been recorded—and the horror he felt is included in the 'programme' of his symphony, which became in turns a tribute and an indictment according to the state of his feelings. He sought what he calls in his Memoirs a 'violent distraction.' Her name was Marie-Félicité-Denise Moke, but she was commonly known as 'Camille' Moke and afterwards she became a famous pianist as Mme Camille Pleyel. Ferdinand Hiller, who was in love with her, asked Berlioz to be his intermediary, with the result that he was supplanted. Berlioz called her his 'Ariel,' and after some rebuffs succeeded in obtaining her mother's consent to their engagement.

Italian Days

In October, 1830, the time arrived for the official performance of 'Sardanapale,' to which the composer had meanwhile added the all-important final conflagration, but although it had been duly rehearsed, the horns missed a vital cue, the percussion, relying upon them, were afraid to 'come in' and the whole effect was a failure. The composer was so mortified that he flung the score at the orchestra and created a scandal. To retrieve the catastrophe he gave another concert at the Conservatoire on 5th December, the programme of which comprised, among other works, both 'Sardanapale' and the 'Symphonie Fantastique.' It was to pillory Miss Smithson's turpitude, but of this she remained blissfully unaware. Meanwhile, on 7th November, at a benefit concert, there had been performed a *fantaisie dramatique* with chorus, on Shakespeare's *The Tempest*, a work that subsequently became the final section of 'Lélio.' At the end of the year he left for La Côte to spend a few weeks with his parents, during which he was much troubled by the silence of his fiancée, and in February he set out from Lyons for the obligatory sojourn in Rome.

It may be expedient to review his position as a composer at this date. Too often has it been said that he arrived in Paris in a state of raw ignorance. As a matter of fact he had studied with good effect, and knew theoretically far more than has commonly been credited to him. What he lacked was mainly experience. He had heard next to nothing. This, however, he quickly remedied on his arrival even before his meeting with Lesueur, by attending performances at the opera and elsewhere and by assiduously studying scores at the Conservatoire library, which he knew so thoroughly that his ejaculations over inaccuracies at public performances became notorious. To refer to him as ill equipped for his tasks is to fly in the face of facts. Heterodox his knowledge may have been, but it was extensive and thorough. By the time he left for Rome he had written an immense quantity of music, much of which he destroyed, retaining what he considered to be of value for incorporation in later works. The surviving compositions included the original version of 'Faust,' the two overtures, 'Waverley' and 'Les Francs Juges,' 'La Mort de Cléopâtre,' the 'Irish Melodies' and the 'Symphonie Fantastique'—quite enough to make of him the outstanding figure in French music of his day.

The route chosen by Berlioz for his journey to Italy was an unusual one. Having no desire to attempt the crossing of the Alps in winter, he travelled first to Marseilles, where he spent a few days waiting for a ship. Eventually he fell in with some young fellows who had arranged to cross to Leghorn on a Sardinian brig. They had to provide their own food, and were not unwilling that he should 'mess' with them. They encountered terrible weather. The journey which should have taken five days took eleven, three of which were spent in sight of Nice, where a head wind made progress impossible. Happily Berlioz was a good sailor and enjoyed the experience. Among his fellow passengers was a Venetian who claimed to have commanded Byron's corvette during the poet's adventures in the Adriatic and the Greek islands. The composer confesses that he was much too pleased to find himself in the company of a man who had possibly shared Childe Harold's Pilgrimage to question his veracity. It was this experience that gave him the original idea of his overture 'The Corsair,' of which he wrote the first version the following year in Rome. He duly arrived at the Villa Medici, then under the direction of the painter Horace Vernet, where they had almost ceased to expect him, and was received with great hilarity by the students. The following day he made the acquaintance of Mendelssohn, his relations with whom appear somewhat strange in the light of their correspondence. Berlioz wrote to his Paris friends that he thought Mendelssohn to be one of the greatest musical intellects of the day, a fine fellow, and 'one of those frank beings whom one so rarely meets.' Mendelssohn wrote to his mother that Berlioz was a caricature without a shadow of talent, groping in the darkness but with boundless conceit. Another famous musician whom he met in Rome was Glinka, the father of modern Russian music. He, at all events, was a kindred soul.

Berlioz had still no news of his fiancée, Mlle. Moke, but indirectly he heard rumours impugning her fidelity. Quite suddenly he decided to return home and learn the truth. He was detained at Florence by a sore throat and, on collecting his letters, found among them one from his prospective mother-in-law overwhelming him with vague reproaches and announcing her daughter's marriage to Camille Pleyel. In a jealous rage he resolved to hasten to Paris to 'kill two guilty women and an innocent man,' but as news of his approach might reach them he first procured as a disguise the attire of a lady's maid. But in changing coaches at Pietra Santa he lost his disguise and had to wait at Genoa while another was being made. This gave time for reflection, with the result that he proceeded no further than Nice, whence, after a few pleasant weeks, during which he composed the overture to 'King Lear,' he retraced his steps. On the way back to Rome he composed 'Lélio,' incorporating in it fragments of earlier works, with the Fantasy on Shakespeare's 'The Tempest' as concluding movement. In Rome he composed 'The Corsair' and 'Rob Roy' overtures and one or two minor works. He left on 1st May, 1832, and arrived at Grenoble on 31st May on his way to La Côte. His sojourn in Italy had brought him little but boredom. He had no liking for the music he heard and spent his time rambling over the country-side, gathering impressions that were to fructify later in 'Harold in Italy.' He became sufficiently interested in Horace Vernet's daughter to refuse the heiress his father had meanwhile found him, but soon forgot her afterwards. He spent some time in the Dauphiné revising various works, and did not reach Paris until 6th November, when he found accommodation in an apartment which happened to have been previously occupied by Miss Smithson. Possibly this association rekindled his flame for her, which blazed up anew.

Married Life

On 9th December Berlioz gave a concert of his works at the Conservatoire. The Programme included the overture of 'Les Francs Juges,' the 'Symphonie Fantastique,' of which the literary basis had been so modified as to become once more a tribute to the actress, and its sequel, 'Lélio,' or 'The Return of Life.' Bocage, a famous actor, declaimed the monologues of the latter and the concert was such a success that it was repeated within the month. By the intermediary of Schlesinger, the original publisher of his 'Faust,' Berlioz had sent an invitation to Harriet Smithson, who attended the concert and was so touched at finding herself the heroine of a great dramatic work that at last she consented to meet him. The actress had begun a season on 21st November with her own company, first at the *Théâtre Italien* where four performances were given, and then at other theatres. But the novelty of the English players had worn off, and the venture was a ruinous failure. By 30th March, when the season petered out completely, Miss Smithson was in dire straits. She was entirely without means and owed 14,000 francs. As an additional misfortune, during the preparations of a concert for her benefit she broke her leg whilst alighting from a carriage. At this time Berlioz was constantly proving his devotion, and alternating between extremes of hope and despair during which he even threatened suicide in her presence. It is small wonder that, probably against her better judgment, Harriet eventually yielded. They were married on 3rd October, 1833, at the British Embassy, in the face of violent objections from both families.

Whatever chances there may have been of the marriage proving a success were probably ruined by the material position of the couple. Harriet was not merely a waning star. Her stage career was practically at an end. Despite two benefit performances she was not clear of debt, and her attempts to recover her popularity were in vain. Berlioz on his wedding day possessed 300 francs. He had long been a musical journalist, and he now wrote more copiously than ever, besides giving concerts, but although he came to be recognised as one of the most brilliant of critics, his earnings were long precarious. Meanwhile Harriet was gradually becoming embittered at her own failure as a contributor to the family fortunes. Her temper grew shrewish and undermined Berlioz's affection whilst at the same time hers, which had at first been rather cool, developed into a jealous passion. She also became self-indulgent and began to lose her good looks. Scenes were frequent and her stage experience helped her to make them effective. Berlioz appears to have held out for some time, but towards the end of 1841, he became acquainted with Marie Martin, professionally known as Marie Recio, and in September, 1842, when he left for his first foreign tour, it was in her company.

Paganini

During those nine years the composer's fame had spread through Europe, enhanced by important new works. The first of these was the symphony, 'Harold in Italy.' After one of his concerts, given on 22nd December, 1833, at which the 'Symphonie Fantastique' had been performed, he was stopped in the corridor by 'a man with long hair, piercing eyes, a strange and haggard face, a genius, a Titan among the giants.' This was Paganini, whom he had not previously met, and who pressed his hand, overwhelming him with praise of the work. He had recently acquired a Stradivarius viola, which he was anxious to play in public. With that purpose in view he called on Berlioz and requested him to write a work for viola and orchestra. Berlioz warned him that such a work as he would write was not likely to be what a virtuoso required, but Paganini insisted, and he wrote the first movement of a then nameless symphony, with a viola solo, using for the purpose a theme from the 'Rob Roy' overture which he intended discarding. As he expected, Paganini was dissatisfied. There were too many rests for the soloist. He must be playing the whole time. A few days later Paganini left for Nice, and the two did not meet for three years, but Berlioz did not abandon his symphony. Drawing upon his Italian memories he made of the viola a kind of melancholy dreamer, after the manner of Byron's 'Childe Harold' and called the symphony 'Harold in Italy.' It was first performed at the Conservatoire on 23rd November, 1834, but Paganini did not hear it until 16th December, 1838. Two days later he wrote Berlioz an enthusiastic letter, enclosing a draft upon Messrs. Rothschild for the sum of twenty thousand francs. This munificent and unexpected gift was the means of relieving the composer of his immediate necessities and thereby providing him with the requisite leisure for the composition of his 'Romeo and Juliet' symphony, so that we are indebted to Paganini for the incentive to two of Berlioz's greatest compositions.

The Siege of the 'Opéra'

Berlioz did not share the views of his countrymen, who held at that time, and long afterwards, that a composer could not be deemed great until he had triumphed in opera. He declared that 'music has huge wings which she can never unfold to their fullest extent within the walls of a theatre.' Nevertheless he was far from desiring to exclude opera from the scope of his ambitions. In 1834 he accepted a libretto written for him by Léon de Wailly and Auguste Barbier on the subject of Benvenuto Cellini, and the three of them submitted it to the Opéra Comique, but it was rejected. Then began a siege of the Opéra, conducted in the Press and behind the scenes, which lasted until the beginning of 1837. The management agreed at last, after the production of two works that it had in prospect, to perform Berlioz's opera, upon which he had begun to work during the previous year. He had been since 1835 the musical critic of the *Journal des Débats*, in which capacity he praised an opera 'Esmeralda,' by Louise Angélique Bertin, whose father owned the newspaper. He was even accused of having helped her in the composition of the work, a charge that he vigorously denied, but it can be readily imagined to what use the insinuation was put in the Press campaign which raged round the name of Berlioz. He had, however, completed his opera by April, 1837, except the overture, which was added when production appeared imminent.

Meanwhile he had succeeded in obtaining from the Ministry of the Interior a commission to compose a Requiem Mass for the second anniversary of the funeral of victims of 28th July, 1835, when Fieschi's attempt on the life of King Louis-Philippe had resulted in the death, among others, of Marshal Mortier. Thus originated the famous 'Messe des Morts,' one of Berlioz's greatest works. It was, however, attended by the ill-luck that seemed to pursue all the composer's achievements. A few days before the anniversary it was officially announced that the religious ceremony would not take place, and for a time it appeared as if Berlioz had laboured in vain. But in October news reached Paris of the fall of Constantine, Algeria, which had cost the lives of General de Damrémont and many officers and men. The King ordered that the General should be buried in the Invalides, and that the ceremony should commemorate the brave men who had fallen with him. The Requiem being ready, it was performed on 5th December, 1837. Even then Berlioz experienced some difficulty in obtaining payment.

On 10th September, 1838, after many set-backs, at last 'Benvenuto Cellini' was produced at the *Opéra* where it achieved what the composer ruefully called *une chute éclatante*. The overture was received with acclamations, but there success ended, though an analysis of contemporary reports shows that the reason lay rather in the libretto, the stage production and the performance than in the music itself. But the nature of these reports was such as to keep away the public, and for the time being 'Benvenuto Cellini' shared the fate of many operas which have failed because they were not given the time and support needed for success. The overture, however, quickly established itself in the repertoire. To Berlioz this failure to win the opera public was a cruel blow. He had counted upon 'Benvenuto Cellini' to give his reputation that lustre which in the France of his day only a successful opera could bestow.

Four performances were given of the opera. The last having been delayed by a change in the cast, Berlioz was not left disconsolate at its withdrawal, for it was then that the concert took place which prompted Paganini's munificence. This enabled him now to begin immediately his next important work, the vast symphony 'Romeo and Juliet,' a project that had haunted his imagination ever since the first days of his Shakespearean enthusiasm. He began it on 24th January, 1839, and by 8th September the score was completed. The first performance took place under his direction in the Hall of the Conservatoire on 24th November with an orchestra of 160 players, besides three soloists and a chorus of 98 for the vocal sections. Two further performances followed in rapid succession, which is no mean tribute to a work of this character.

Throughout his career Berlioz formed vast projects and had to wait for the opportunity to present itself for their realisation. Sometimes the opportunity came, as in the case of the Requiem. More often than not he was disappointed. One such project was the music of a huge commemorative festival in honour of France's famous men. Two sections of it were already in existence in 1835, and the 'Te Deum' of 1849 is said to have been a tardy contribution to the realisation of the same cherished idea. Officially, however, it is represented by the 'Symphonie Funèbre et Triomphale' for chorus and orchestra, commissioned by the Ministry of the Interior for the inauguration on 28th July, 1840, tenth anniversary of the revolution of 1830, of the column erected on the Place de la Bastille. At the original performance the orchestra of 200 was of wind instruments only, but at a subsequent concert it was performed by a combined military band of 120 and symphonic orchestra of 130. This is the work of which Wagner, who was then living in Paris, speaks so highly in his autobiography. It is also the last work of any importance that Berlioz composed before he entered upon the wanderings which occupied his later years. Towards the end of 1841 he formed the liaison mentioned above with Marie Recio. She was engaged at the *Opéra*—it is said, on Berlioz's recommendation—but without much success. If ever he had any illusion concerning her talent as a singer it was soon dispelled, for we know on the authority of Hiller that her ambition to sing at his concerts was a sore trial to him. But his critical susceptibilities did not moderate his ardour. Harriet, his first wife, died on 3rd March, 1853, and on 19th October, 1854, he married Marie Recio. It does not seem that this second marriage proved any happier than the first. If, however, contemporaries do not speak well of the second Madame Berlioz, they have nothing but praise for her Spanish mother, Mme Martin, *née* Sotera de Villas, who would appear to have flown in the face of all 'mother-in-law' tradition by watching with devoted care over Berlioz's welfare. If we have taken a leap forward in Berlioz's biography, it is because it is the last occasion on which we shall have occasion to refer to his domestic life.

A Musician's Wanderings

Berlioz's first spell of foreign travel opened with a visit to Brussels in September, 1842, when he conducted several of his works. He had already planned his German tour, but returned first to Paris for a great farewell concert which took place on 7th November. The same month an election was held at the Académie des Beaux-Arts to fill the vacancy created by the death of Cherubini, the preceding March. There were five candidates: Onslow, Adam, Berlioz, Zimmermann, and Dourlen, of whom Adam complacently records that only the first two merited serious consideration. Of these Onslow proved successful, which must have been a bitter disappointment to the composer of 'Giselle,' the successful ballet produced a year earlier. Berlioz left Paris again in December and travelled to Germany *via* Brussels. He was unable to give the projected concerts at Mainz or Frankfurt and continued his journey to Stuttgart where, on 29th December, he conducted a programme of his symphonic works in the presence of the King and the Court. This was followed by concerts at Weimar, Leipzig, Brunswick, Hamburg, Berlin, and Darmstadt, whence he returned to Paris at the end of May, 1843.

One of the works he had taken with him on his travels was his unfortunate opera 'Benvenuto Cellini.' Turning over the pages he concluded that there were ideas in it worth saving from the wreck. With that end in view he wrote a new 'ouverture caractéristique,' intended to be a separate work, which he entitled 'Le Carnaval Romain' and dedicated to one of his new-found German patrons, the Prince of Hohenzollern-Hechingen. Eventually, however, it became a second overture to the opera, in which it precedes the second act. That winter and the following spring Berlioz conducted several concerts in Paris, at one of which, on 3rd February, 1844, he conducted the first performance of 'Le Carnaval Romain.' The principal composition upon which he was then engaged was an opera, 'La Nonne Sanglante,' begun two years earlier and intended for the *Opéra* but destined to remain unfinished. In August, 1844, however, he went to Nice to recuperate after the fatigues of the season, and occupied a tower near the Rocher des Ponchettes; possibly the scene recalled his experiences of 1831, when he was weather-bound in sight of Nice on his way to Rome, for he rewrote the overture, 'The Corsair,' in which he had recorded his impressions. This new version was entitled 'La Tour de Nice,' and performed on 13th January, 1845, at the first of four concerts arranged by Franconi at the *Cirque des Champs-Élysées*, when it proved a failure. He destroyed the score, but evidently still possessed the original version, for ten years later he again rewrote it. This final version was first performed by the Société Sainte-Cécile, on 1st April, 1855. It was then announced as 'The Red Corsair,' but on publication the adjective was dropped and the original title restored. Though well received at the time, this work afterwards suffered neglect until it was taken up by Hans von Bülow, who included it in his programmes when touring with the Meiningen Orchestra. After the spring season of 1845 Berlioz again recuperated in the South during June and July. In August he attended the unveiling of the Beethoven monument at Bonn, returning to Paris almost immediately to prepare for his second extended tour.

Faust

He left at the end of October and arrived in Vienna on 3rd November. As on his former journey he was accompanied by Marie Recio, but he appears to have subdued her determination to sing, for the programme of one of his first concerts in Vienna shows another artist singing 'Le Pâtre Breton,' which on the previous tour she had considered as reserved for her. What is, however, more important, is that on this journey he took with him his 'Eight Scenes from Faust,' which were to be incorporated in a larger work. In the Memoirs he writes: 'Whilst trailing round Germany in my old postchaise I composed my "Damnation of Faust." Each movement is punctuated by memories of the place where it was written. For instance the Peasants' Dance was jotted down by the light of a shop gas-jet one night when I had lost myself in Budapest, and I got up in the middle of the night at Prague to write the song of the angelic choir.' Other portions were composed on the Danube steamers. At Vienna Berlioz met many friends, one of whom—possibly Liszt—lent him a collection of Hungarian national airs, among which was that of the 'Rakoczy March.' He was so attracted by the tune that in one night he made the now well-known orchestral version subsequently incorporated in 'Faust.' He had it with him when, after directing concerts at Vienna and Prague, he proceeded to the Hungarian capital. At that time, in the restless forties, the atmosphere there was heavily charged with political electricity. A storm was brewing which was to burst out later. In the circumstances it is not surprising to read in the composer's Memoirs that the first performance of this march made a volcanic impression on an audience of patriots. The occasion became, in fact, a patriotic demonstration. He records: 'The extraordinary effect it produced at Budapest induced me to introduce it in "Faust" by taking the liberty of placing my hero in Hungary at the beginning of the action.' The next stage of the tour was Breslau, after which he conducted another concert at Prague, revisited Brunswick and returned to Paris at the beginning of May, 1846.

Back in France, and whilst still engaged upon the last remaining portions of 'Faust,' he composed a choral work, 'Le Chant des Chemins de Fer,' which was performed at Lille, 14th June, 1846, the occasion being the inauguration of that railway which is so well-known to English travellers, the *Chemin de Fer du Nord*. 'Faust' was finished on 19th October and performed for the first time on 6th December at the *Opéra Comique*, which was not more than half-filled. A second performance fared no better, and the composer found himself seriously in debt. Friends, however, came to his assistance and he was able to leave Paris, 14th February, 1847, on his first visit to Russia, where he gave successful concerts at St. Petersburg, Moscow and Riga. He broke his homeward journey at the request of the King of Prussia, who wished to hear his 'Faust.' He reached Paris on 4th June, and in August received an offer from Jullien, who had just taken Drury Lane Theatre, to come to London and conduct the opera. He arrived on 5th November, and stayed at 76 Harley Street. The opera opened on 6th December with Donizetti's 'Lucia di Lammermoor,' but only two other works were presented, and the undertaking failed at the end of four months, owing chiefly to Jullien's extravagance. Berlioz gave two concerts in London, one on 7th February, the other on 29th June, 1848, but the receipts did not go far to compensate him for Jullien's failure. He left London on 16th July, bringing back with him the first instalment of his Memoirs and a version for female chorus of his 'Ballade sur la Mort d'Ophélie,' dated 4th July. Soon after his arrival in Paris his father died, on 26th July, and he had to journey to La Côte to settle up his affairs. Whilst there he visited all the familiar places haunted with memories of his childhood, and learned that his once-beloved Estelle was now fifty-one, a widow with a grown-up son at the Bar. Returning to Paris he composed, on 22nd September, the impressive 'Marche Funèbre' for the last scene of *Hamlet*.

The 'Te Deum' and 'L'Enfance du Christ'

Meanwhile the revolution of February had resulted in the abdication of King Louis-Philippe and the establishment of a Republic. On 20th December Prince Louis Napoleon was elected President. It was at this time that Berlioz planned another large work, in honour of the first Napoleon. It was to be entitled 'Le Retour de la Campagne d'Italie,' and at the entrance of the victorious general Bonaparte into the cathedral a 'Te Deum' was to resound through the sacred building. Thus originated another of those works for State occasions which Berlioz found so hard afterward to place. When in 1852 Louis Napoleon abolished the Constitution and became the Emperor Napoleon III, the composer hoped that this 'Te Deum' might be used at his coronation. The following year he hoped it might be used for his wedding. Again disappointed, he tried to have it commissioned for the opening of the Paris Exhibition of 1855. That it was performed on the eve of that event was, however, due not to the Government, which again failed him, but to Ducroquet, the organ builder, who had installed the previous year a new instrument in the Church of St. Eustache, and persuaded a few friends to join him in guaranteeing the expenses. The 'Te Deum' was then published, with a dedication to the Prince Consort. It is one of Berlioz's greatest works, but it had to wait nearly six years for a performance.

In January, 1850, Berlioz founded the *Société Philharmonique* of Paris which gave its first concert on 19th February and, alas, its last on 25th March, 1851. At one of the concerts of its second season, on 12th November, 1850, it gave the first performance of 'La Fuite en Égypte,' fragment of an oratorio ostensibly by Pierre Ducré, maître de chapelle at the Sainte Chapelle in 1679, but in reality by Berlioz himself and destined to become the central portion of his sacred trilogy, 'L'Enfance du Christ,' afterwards known in England as 'The Holy Family.' The two sections which were added later are the first, 'Le Songe d'Hérode,' and the third 'L'Arrivée à Saïs.' The completed trilogy was performed for the first time on 10th December, 1854. It bears a dedication to John Ella, founder and director of the Musical Union in London, which the composer had visited three times in the interval since the trilogy was begun. The first occasion was an official one in connection with the great Exhibition of 1851 in Hyde Park. He left Paris on 9th May and stayed at 27 Queen Anne Street, Cavendish Square. It was then that he first became associated with Dr. Henry Wylde, professor at the Royal Academy, and T. W. Beale, a partner in the firm of Cramer, who secured his services for their projected New Philharmonic Society, which was founded in January, 1852. He returned, and conducted the first concert of the society on 24th March, four days after Liszt had presented, and incidentally rehabilitated, his 'Benvenuto Cellini' at Weimar. Six concerts were given that season, the last on 9th June. The financial outcome was unsatisfactory and Berlioz was not re-engaged until 1855, but the guarantors persevered and the society lasted until 1879, when its concerts were taken over by William Ganz.

More Wanderings

November 1852 found Berlioz at Weimar, where a week's festival was held of his works, including the performances of 'Benvenuto Cellini,' which was produced by Liszt on 20th March. It was one of Berlioz's greatest triumphs. The following spring he returned to London where he conducted his 'Harold in Italy' at the sixth concert of the (now Royal) Philharmonic Society, and a fortnight later, on 25th June, his 'Benvenuto Cellini' was produced under his direction, for the only time at Covent Garden. According to Spohr, who was present, the audience 'broke out into one general storm of hisses and whistling, a circumstance never before known to have occurred at the Italian Opera in London in the presence of the Queen.' For some of this an Italian element in the audience appears to have been responsible. A supper had been arranged to take place after the performance and many distinguished guests were invited, but after the catastrophe they were reluctant to meet the victim, and failed to attend with the exception of J. W. Davison, musical critic of The Times, with whom Berlioz dined in what his companion afterwards described as a sentimental tête-à-tête. Efforts were made to atone to him for this failure, but the mischief was done and the opera was never again performed in London.

A month after his return from London, Berlioz left for Baden-Baden on the invitation of Bénazet, the lessee of the Casino. It was the first of a series of visits that were to continue annually and lead eventually to the composition of an opera, his last, 'Béatrice et Bénédict.' In 1855 he paid another visit to London at the invitation of the New Philharmonic. This was the season when Wagner conducted the concerts of the senior Philharmonic. He also paid repeated visits to Weimar, and occasionally to other German cities, but his attention was soon to become absorbed in another great work, 'Les Troyens,' in which his devotion to Virgil was to find expression. Whilst at Weimar in February 1856 he discussed the plan of this work, based on the second and fourth books of the Æneid, with the Princess Sayn-Wittgenstein, who gave him every encouragement. He kept her informed and reported to her on 24th June that the libretto was nearly ready. Two years later the music was completed. It is a vast opera, in two parts, 'La Prise de Troie' and 'Les Troyens à Carthage,' of which the latter was produced separately at the *Théâtre Lyrique*, 4th November, 1863. The first part was not performed in the composer's lifetime, and the first integral performance of the whole work did not take place until Felix Mottl gave it at Karlsruhe on two evenings, 6th and 7th December, 1890.

The Last Work

In August, 1858, Bénazet told Berlioz of his intention to build a theatre at Baden-Baden. He wanted to commission an opera on an episode of the Thirty Years War, but the subject bore too much resemblance to 'Les Francs Juges' and the composer suggested 'Béatrice et Bénédict,' based on Shakespeare's *Much Ado about Nothing*. The composition was begun towards the end of 1859, and completed early in 1862. The opera was produced in the new theatre on 9th August, 1862, and eight months later at Weimar, but not in

Paris until after the composer's death. It was to prove his last work. He paid a few more visits to Germany and Austria, and one to Russia in the winter of 1867–8, at the invitation of the Grand Duchess Helena. It was another great triumph, culminating in a banquet on his birthday which was attended by five hundred people. But he was already a sick man and his death on 8th March, 1869, occasioned little surprise. His only son had died at Havana, of yellow fever, in 1867, his second wife five years earlier. During those last few years he found solace in corresponding with the Estelle of his youth, now nearing seventy and a grandmother, and even tried to persuade her to marry him. To the end a Romantic! Perhaps one should say *the* Romantic, for it is difficult to name another artist as completely representative of all that is meant by the Romantic Movement.

BIBLIOGRAPHY

BERLIOZ, HECTOR: *Autobiography.* Translated by K. F. BOULT. 2s. (Dent, 'Everyman's Library,' 1923.)

BOSCHOT, ADOLPHE: *L'Histoire d'un Romantique.* 2 vols. (Paris, 1908–13.)

CONSTANTIN, LÉON: *Berlioz.* (Paris, 1934.)

COQUARD, ARTHUR: *Berlioz.* (Paris, 'Musiciens Célèbres,' 1909.)

KAPP, JULIUS: *Berlioz.* (Berlin, 1922.)

MASSON, P. M.: *Berlioz.* (Paris, 'Maîtres de la Musique,' 1923.)

PROD'HOMME, J.-G.: *Hector Berlioz, sa Vie et ses Œuvres.* (Paris, 1913.)

TURNER, W. J.: *Berlioz, the Man and his Music.* 10s. 6d. (Dent, 1935.)

WOTTON, TOM S.: *Hector Berlioz.* 7s. 6d. (Oxford University Press, 1935.)

FRÉDÉRIC FRANÇOIS CHOPIN

BORN 22 February 1810   DIED 17 October 1849

By Herbert Hughes

Poland and Lorraine

There are people, some of them solemn musicologists, who regard Chopin as a creative artist of the second rank. He is not, they say, colossal; therefore he cannot be ranked with composers of the calibre of, for example, Bach or Beethoven. That is a questionable sort of estimation. Æsthetic values have surely nothing to do with size, though quantity may imply influence, as influence implies power. Must one be impressed by the Pyramids of Gizeh? I do not intend to discuss here the paradox that colossalism is often an expression of the little mind, but to suggest that the relatively frail, sensitive Chopin, expressing himself in unpretentious forms, less ostensibly intellectual than the symphonists, less spectacular than the composers of opera, was one of the greatest forces in modern music and probably not less vital than his great contemporaries, Beethoven and Schubert. It is not merely that the influence of his original mind can be traced in the music of Liszt, Wagner, Schumann, Tchaikovsky, Grieg, Wolf, Scriabin, Debussy, Delius and a host of smaller writers in between, but that it is to be found in the music—good and bad—that is heard on the radio every day of our lives. That influence has been not merely academic, not merely world-wide, but domestic and remains incalculable.

His ancestry was mixed: French on his father's side,
Polish on his mother's. It is now established that his father
Nicolas (born in 1771), his grandfather François (a wheelwright who became a vine-grower), and his great-grand-
father Nicolas were natives of Lorraine. At his father's
baptism in the parish of Diarville one of the witnesses was
Thérèse Chopin, of Xirocourt, a spinster and presumably a
relative, who was unable to write, and observed the regulations by marking with a cross the entry in the parish
register.

Modern Lorraine is but a fraction of that *Lotharii
regnum* (Lothringen), a vast territory extending from the
shores of the North Sea to the centre of Italy, taking in
the Netherlands, Rhinelands, Switzerland and Lombardy,
which by the Treaty of Verdun, A.D. 843, was allotted to
the eldest of Charlemagne's grandsons, Lothaire II. Celtic,
Roman and German blood had contributed to the main
stream of Lorraine's population through a long period
of history. The overlordship of the province itself had
been disputed over and over again; German and Frankish
kings had fought for possession; and there followed by
the successive treaties of Cateau-Cambrésis 1559, Westphalia
1648, Pyrenees 1659, Nymwegen 1679, Ryswick 1697,
and Vienna 1738 such an international buffeting that it
would be unnatural if partisanship had not coloured its historical records and literature. After the Franco-Prussian war
of 1870–71, German ethnologists were found to stress
the Germanic influences that had persisted since Cæsar's
time, while French scholars dwelt on qualities of non-
Teutonic character. The disputants are still articulate.
In the circumstances it may well be left to later writers,
with possibly more material than is now available, to
discuss the various spellings of Chopin, Choppen, and
Schopen, and to delve further into the family history of
a composer whose paternal ancestors came from such an
epic battlefield.

c

A Lorrainer Comes to Poland

It is known that the composer's father, Nicolas—brown-eyed, intelligent, vivacious—was about seventeen when he was persuaded by a friend in Warsaw, who owned a small tobacco and snuff manufactory, to emigrate thither and take a post in the counting-house, an apprenticeship that was probably humdrum enough until political upheaval brought it to an end. Nicolas was in his twenty-third year when Poland, in 1794, went through another paroxysm of her turbulent history. Kosciuszko called his compatriots to arms; trade was upset; and the tobacco and snuff establishment had to close down. Nicolas, although not robust, was spirited enough to join the National Guard and was soon promoted captain. In November the Russians made a furious and successful assault on the suburb of Praga, which had been in a state of siege. Captain Nicolas Chopin and his company happened to be relieved a few hours before the collapse of the position, to which providential circumstance he, no doubt, owed his life. But Warsaw fell and the career of Nicolas as a temporary officer came to an end.

On two occasions Nicolas was on the point of returning to his native Lorraine, and on each he was deflected from doing so by indifferent health. Then there came a day when he met the Staorcina Laczynska, who was so struck by his intelligence and character that she immediately engaged him as tutor in the French language to her four children. That engagement lasted until the children had grown up, and was succeeded by another similar post in the family of the Countess Skarbek at Zelazowa Zola, an estate about 28 miles outside Warsaw. There he met and loved Justina Krzyzanowska, companion and lady-in-waiting, and married her with the blessings of the Countess. Justina, we are told, was twenty-four and the daughter of a noble Polish family that had suffered impoverishment; but of the family history little or nothing appears to be known. The marriage, however, was a happy one, and on 22nd February,

1810, the composer was born, the second of four children and the only son. He was baptized Frédéric François, his godmother being Countess Anne Skarbek, and his godfather her brother, Count Fryderyk Skarbek, a youth of seventeen.

The composer's close association with the aristocracy, begun thus early, was to continue throughout his life and to have a profound effect upon his work and his outlook. Shortly after he was born his parents transferred their home to Warsaw, where his father was appointed to a professorship of French in the newly opened Lycée; and while he accepted other similar appointments at the School of Artillery and Engineering, at the Preparatory Military Academy, and the Academy of the Roman Catholic Clergy, he set up a boarding school 'for the sons of the Nobility and Gentry.' This last was Frédéric's only 'prep.' school, and he spent some years there before proceeding to the Lycée. Poets, artists, men of science were among his father's intimates, and it was in an atmosphere of culture and refinement that he spent his first impressionable years. Of the composer's mother little is recorded. George Sand, who never met her, said in her sententious way that she was Chopin's only passion. Karasowski, who must have known her well, described her as being particularly tender-hearted and rich in all fine womanly qualities, finding the greatest happiness in 'quietness and homeliness.' Niecks recorded the remark of a Scots lady who had seen Justina Chopin in her old age, and talked with her in French, that she was 'a neat, quiet, intelligent old lady.' A prosaic phrase that carries in it —when one considers to whom it was applied—the whole mystery of motherhood, the motherhood of genius.

The Wand of Youth

No creative artist who ever lived had a happier childhood than Frédéric Chopin. The atmosphere of his home was serene and sympathetic; there was no element in it that could be regarded as antagonistic to the free development of his mind. He was not robust, neither was he remarkably delicate; he played games, and was, of course, somewhat precocious in his flair for music, though not exceptionally so. When he was an infant the sound of music made him weep, yet before he could read or write he had already begun to take pianoforte lessons from a Bohemian fiddler and pedagogue, Adalbert Zywny. Before he could handle a pen he had begun to compose, his master writing down his childish efforts, putting them straight, and telling him of a composer called Bach, whom he worshipped—whom Frédéric, too, was soon to worship. The boy was boisterous and dreamy in turn, droll, high-spirited, delighting in mimicry. And his musical gifts developed apace. Practical jokes and private theatricals alternated with the creation of little valses and mazurkas and polonaises. By the time he was eight years old his talents were discussed beyond the family circle.

On the eve of his ninth birthday Frédéric was waited on by Niemcewicz, the illustrious statesman and *littérateur*, on behalf of several leaders of Warsaw society inviting him to take part in a concert that was being organised for charity. At this *début*—for it was his first public concert—he took the solo part in a piano concerto by the eminent composer, Adalbert Gyrowetz, and with such success that the leaders of Warsaw society were soon in open competition to pet and entertain, and be entertained by, such a wonder-child. Only the calm mental discipline of his methodical home, and his already acute sense of humour—humour that in later life was to become bitter and sardonic on occasion—prevented such praise and adulation going to his head. Invitations came from the princely houses of Czartoryski, Radziwill, Sapieha, Lubecki, and others of the local aristocracy. The Princess Czetwertynska, whose drawing-room was a particular rendezvous of artists and elegant amateurs, took him to the Princess Lowicka, the Polish wife of the Grand Duke

Constantine, the 'Napoleon of Belvedere,' and Frédéric was soon a familiar little figure at the ducal palace as playmate to Paul, the Grand Duke's son, a boy of his own age.

When he entered the Lycée at the age of fifteen his music had to be studied outside school hours, and under the guidance of Joseph Elsner, Director of the Conservatoire. Elsner, famed as a church musician and teacher, at once perceived the rare qualities, expressed and latent, in the poetic boy who came to him for lessons in harmony and counterpoint —a boy with silken auburn hair, beautiful hands, and the sloping shoulders of a girl. He put Frédéric under no restraint that could curb his imagination; rather did he show him—if that was necessary—what it meant to be exacting to oneself. Frédéric's schooling had sharpened a naturally keen intelligence, and Elsner found a disciplined and lively young mind to work upon, a mind surprisingly radiant under the veil of languid eyes.

Early Influences

To an intelligent and imaginative boy with such an upbringing in such surroundings it was inevitable that the literary movements of the day should be familiar at least by repute. The classicism that had survived the eighteenth century was in decay, though dying hard. Poland was in a state of intellectual renaissance. Romanticism was almost in full flower, already tinging the study of political history and folk-lore. Now and then Frédéric would join his father on excursions into the country, and it may easily be assumed that into their conversations would slip the names—often discussed by his father's guests—of Mickiewicz (whose verse was bringing a new note into Polish literature) and Goethe and Jean Jacques Rousseau, of Schiller and that young Englishman, Byron, who had joined the Greek army and had lately died at Missolonghi; names strangely mixed, maybe, with those of Bach and Mozart and that excellent pianist,

Carl Maria von Weber, whose 'Freischütz' had been seen in Warsaw. With the widespread and deliberate cult of nationalism went naturally the collection and preservation of folk-songs; and Frédéric took delight in listening to these in their native environment. Art-music, a thing of the cities and the courts, had not yet affected the traditional music and dances of the country-side; and the mind of the adolescent student was strangely moved when he became aware that all that enchanting beauty of rhythm and melodic line was the ancient and expressive birthright of a peasantry incredibly ignorant and superstitious. And in his attic at dead of night, while improvising mazurkas and krakowiaks and polonaises on the piano in rhythm that had been beating into his brain all day, he would make experiments in touch and in the fingering of broken chords, that were to crystallise later on into a technique inseparable from his art, a technique that was to revolutionise the whole art of piano music.

Meanwhile Frédéric's circle of friends and acquaintances were widening and there was little likelihood of the wheelwright's grandson developing into a type of the raw provincial. In this third decade of the nineteenth century the *salons* of the Polish nobility were at the zenith of their brilliance. Many of the families were rich and powerful, the political connection with France during the first Empire to some extent influencing the manners and literary taste without destroying the national distinctiveness of class or loosening the conventions of etiquette. The *noblesse*, while insisting on the proprieties, were far from being stiff-necked; any kind of hard artificiality was antipathetic to their Slavonic caste. Gallantry and good manners, conviviality and a deep love of music and of their national dances were outstanding qualities. It was in frequent contact with such an *ambiente*, blended with that of the Conservatoire, that the youthful mind of Frédéric Chopin was being formed, and the innate characteristics of his own already sensitive nature developed and expanded. He was happy in the companionships of his school days. Juljan Fontana, Counts Antony, Casimir and Felix Wodzinski, Titus Woyciechowski and John Matuszynski were among his closest friends. To Titus and to John in after years he was to write some of his most intimate, self-revealing letters.

Frédéric Abroad and in Love

When he left the Lycée at the age of eighteen Frédéric made his first considerable trip abroad. This was brought about by his father's friend, Dr. Jarocki, zoologist and Professor at the Warsaw University, who suggested that Frédéric should accompany him to a conference of experts in Natural Philosophy which was to take place in Berlin, a five-days' journey by coach. Frédéric, with the curiosity of youth, missed little of the parade of life in the German capital; its motley interested him; he haunted the Singakademie and the Opera, and 'discovered' Handel; and his letters to Titus and his family were buoyant and amusing. At the age of nineteen, accompanied by three friends, he went to Vienna and, unperturbed by that critical public, gave two concerts, visiting Prague, Dresden and Breslau on the way home. At the age of nineteen, moreover, he was in love, and from the 'loneliness' of an adoring home circle he unburdened himself to Titus, from whom he could conceal nothing.

'You cannot imagine,' he wrote on 3rd October, 1829, 'how sad Warsaw is to me; and if I did not feel happy with my people I should not like to live here. Oh, how bitter it is to have no one with whom one can share joy and sorrow, how dreadful to feel one's heart oppressed and to be unable to confide in one human being. You know well what I mean. How often do I tell my piano all that I should like to tell to you! . . . Six months have passed and not yet have I exchanged a syllable with her of whom I dream every night. Whilst my thoughts were with her I composed the Adagio of my Concerto, and early this morning she inspired the Valse which I send along with this letter.'

And the more or less unconscious cause of all this emotional disturbance was the charming Constantia Gladkowska, a pupil at the Warsaw Conservatorium.

At that period, on the threshold of manhood, he was obsessed by three great passions: his art, Constantia (whom he did not yet know) and Titus. His passionate friendship for Titus was covetous and jealous as any lover's; no mistress could be more exacting. To the ordinary West European, knowing neither Titus nor Chopin, certain letters to his beloved friend would appear as the epistles of a homosexual, or at any rate of a youth in whom feminine qualities were predominant.

'If I scrawl to-day again so much nonsense it is only in order to remind you that you are as much locked in my heart as ever and that I am still the same Fred. You do not care to be kissed, but to-day you must permit me to do so. . . . I embrace you heartily and kiss you on your lips if you will permit me. . . . Time passes, I must wash myself . . . do not kiss me now . . . but you would not kiss me now in any case—even if I anointed myself with Byzantine oils—unless by magnetic means I forced you to do so. . . . You, my dearest one, do not require my portrait. Believe me, I am always with you, and shall not forget you until the end of my life. . . . You have no idea how much I love you. If only I could prove it to you. What would I not give if I could once right heartily embrace you!' . . .

Nevertheless, the love-lorn youth did not find life insupportable. He protested that he would not spend the winter in Warsaw, having Vienna in mind; but he did. Prince Radziwill and his wife invited him to Berlin, offering him apartments in their palace; but Constantia, the Ideal, evidently held him in thrall for the time being. Later, having sung for him at a local concert, she slipped into marriage with someone else and, it is said, suffered the misery of blindness.

In November, 1830, after much vacillation, he said

good-bye to Warsaw, being accompanied as far as Wola by Elsner and a number of intimate friends. Elsner had written a cantata for the occasion and had secretly rehearsed it with pupils of the Conservatorium. At Wola Frédéric found a banquet prepared in his honour; the cantata was sung, and a silver goblet filled with Polish earth presented to him. 'May you never forget your native land wherever you may go,' someone said to him, handing him the goblet; 'may you never cease to love it with a warm and faithful heart.' And as the carriage rolled away Frédéric Chopin knew he was never to see Warsaw again, nor set foot on Polish soil. But that goblet and the earth in it he was to keep faithfully to the end, as he kept the letters of Constantia Gladkowska.

Titus accompanied Frédéric to Vienna, but revolution broke out in Poland on 30th November and Titus at once departed to join the insurgents. With dramatic suddenness Frédéric found himself alone and homesick. What should he do? Should he follow Titus? In a letter to his family he laid bare his soul; but they urged him to stay where he was, saying that he was 'not strong enough to bear the hardships and fatigue of a soldier's life.' His loneliness and homesickness together became unbearable; and impulsively he hired a carriage and pursued his friend several stages along the road to Warsaw. Yet his mind was not made up; he was irresolute, his courage gave way, and he returned to Vienna. In the following July (1831) he left Vienna, gave a concert in Munich, and was in Stuttgart on his way to Paris when he learned to his horror that Warsaw had fallen to the Russians on 8th September. 'Who could have foreseen such a calamity?' he cried. Out of the agony of his mind he poured forth the Étude in C Minor—No. 12 of Op. 10—'La Révolution'; and in his notebook he wrote: 'The faubourgs fired! Titus and Matuszynski killed, no doubt! Paskewitsch and that dog from Mohilew seizing the town . . . Oh, God, where art Thou? Art Thou there

and dost Thou not avenge Thyself? Art Thou not sated
with murder?— Or art Thou indeed a Muscovite? . . .'

Early Days in Paris

On his arrival in Paris Chopin took rooms at 27 Boulevard
Poissonnière, opposite the Cité Bergère. He carried with
him letters of introduction, and it was not long before he
met Cherubini, head of the Conservatôire and the greatest
musical influence in France. Cherubini was seventy-one
and kept open house. At first he considered the old pedagogue to be expressionless and cold; in one letter he referred
to him as a mummy, but changed his mind as acquaintance
ripened. Cherubini's Monday evening *salons* were crowded,
and there one would meet Meyerbeer and Rossini, Auber and
Halévy (his favourite pupils), Hummel and Kalkbrenner
and Liszt, stars of the platform and the stage. There was
something in the austerity of the Italian, in his calm, severe
idealism, which soon appeared to the young Franco-Pole,
who became so far devoted that he wrote out a fair copy of
one of Cherubini's fugues. He made the acquaintance of
Mendelssohn, who affectionately dubbed him Chopinetto;
of Ferdinand Hiller, Hummel's pupil, who was the first to
play Beethoven's E flat Concerto in Paris; of Baillot, whom
he called the rival of Paganini; and of many others. He
was so impressed by the smooth dexterity of Kalkbrenner's
piano-playing that for a time he considered taking a course
of lessons (at Kalkbrenner's suggestion) but abandoned the
idea (to Kalkbrenner's disgust) and prepared himself for a
public concert. After two postponements, this took place
on 26th February, 1832, in Pleyel's Rooms. It was a failure
financially; the public knew nothing of Chopin, and the
receipts did not cover the expenses. He played a Concerto,
some Nocturnes and Mazurkas. He took part in Kalkbrenner's new work, a 'Marche suivie d'une Polonaise' for
two pianos (a very large one for Kalkbrenner and a little

one for himself) with accompaniment for four others, 'as loud as an orchestra,' played by Hiller, Osborne, Sowinski and Stamati. Chopin was partly amused, partly disgusted at the sextet of pianos, accepting it as the price paid for his *début*. ('An altogether mad idea' was his comment beforehand in a letter to Titus.) Liszt and Mendelssohn were present, both already eminent personages and both greatly impressed by the young man's individuality. Liszt perceived that in his art he combined a new phase of poetic sentiment with 'happy innovations' in form; Mendelssohn, who had heard all about Kalkbrenner's designs upon Chopinetto's career, was delighted with the playing and applauded vigorously; Hiller declared that now there would be no more nonsense talked about the want of technique. The *soirée musicale*, in fact, if not the talk of the town, was a new topic of conversations in the drawing-rooms—for the moment. And the influential Fétis, in an elaborate report in his *Revue Musicale*, remarked, while objecting to 'too much luxuriance in the modulations, disorder in the linking of the phrases,' that there will be found in M. Chopin's inspirations the indication of 'a renewal of forms which may exercise in time a great influence over this branch of the art.'

After a very short period when he was threatened with desperate penury, good fortune smiled upon him, and Chopin began to make a remarkable reputation as a teacher, his pupils almost without exception being aristocratic young ladies moving in the most exclusive society. His life was now practically the life of the *salon*; bohemianism was antipathetic to him; and deep literary or political discussion he avoided; and the only fellow-artists in whom he showed the slightest interest were those, like Liszt or Franchomme or Delacroix, who happened to move in the same restricted circles. He showed the same fastidiousness in the choice of clothes, in the decoration and arrangement of his rooms, as in the composition of some exquisite *fioriture* for a Nocturne —and over these we know he would spend hours and days altering, restoring, correcting, before he was really satisfied.

'I move in the highest circles, among ambassadors, princes, and ministers,' he wrote to his friend Dziewanowski in January, 1833, 'and I know not how I go there, for I did not in any way thrust myself forward. But at present it is for me an absolute necessity, for thence comes, so to speak, good taste . . . To-day I have to give five lessons. You will imagine that I must have made a fortune by this time; but the cabriolet and the white gloves eat the earnings almost entirely, and without these things people would deny my good form. I love the Carlists, hate the Philippists, and am myself a revolutionist. Therefore I don't care for money, but only for friendship—for the preservation of which I earnestly entreat you.' . . .

How characteristic of the man, of the still young man, was this! In spirit a revolutionist, actually something of a sybarite, dependent on the hated Philippists; caring for friendship, loyal, yet by nature eclectic and hypercritical, having only the most theoretical care (and little of that) for the world outside. With Frédéric Chopin the cabriolet and the white gloves were as much a natural inclination as a conscious investment.

In the summer of 1835 Chopin journeyed to Carlsbad to meet his parents whom he had not seen for five years; in September he proceeded to Dresden at the invitation of the Wodzinski family, and fell in love with Marie, then nineteen years of age. The following summer he joined the Wodzin-skis at Marienbad, and his love for Marie was intensified; but Count Wodzinski's domain of fifty thousand acres no doubt represented in Chopin's mind an obstacle of social rank he could not hope to surmount by the simple process of proposing to the owner's daughter. At any rate, he was gently dismissed, and the world was the richer for at least one perfect Valse dedicated to the insincere Marie.

George Sand

Early in 1837 Chopin first encountered George Sand, one of the most remarkable women in history, and life immediately became complicated. He was in his twenty-eighth, she in her thirty-third year—the most conspicuous figure in a *galère* that included Balzac, Heine, Sainte-Beuve and other men distinguished in literature and the arts. The most intemperate fiction could hardly have produced such a type: a voluptuary without vice, who could take delight in recording her erotic impressions; a woman in whom the qualities of compassion, of hypocrisy, of pure motherliness, and of the vampire were grotesquely mixed. Through her veins coursed the blood of kings and courtesans; lights o' love and aristocrats had collaborated in her pedigree; generations of unsanctified unions had brought her into being. She had had many lovers after her unfortunate marriage to Casimir Dudevant; Jules Sandeau (with whom she co-operated in her first novel), Prosper Mérimée, Alfred de Musset, Dr. Pagello, the tutors Pelletan and Malfille, Leroux—and then Chopin. Let those who would understand this tragic *liaison*, and the contrapuntal character of the quarrel that ended it, read the lady's *Un Hiver à Majorque*, her *Histoire de ma Vie*, and her published Letters, and discount much that is obvious embellishment. George Sand saved Chopin's life during those dreary winter months in Majorca, nursed and watched over him with consummate care in circumstances of unusual difficulty. But tuberculosis had set in; and thereafter, at the château of Nohant and in Paris, with intermittent periods of comparative happiness, the composer's life was in decline. Two visits to England were undertaken in misery. He played to the Queen at the Duchess of Sutherland's in 1848; appeared at other important London houses; underwent the indignity of being treated as a mere touring pianist of no account; suffered a complexity of boredom with country-house visits in Scotland, recitals in the provinces, and a certain amount of indifferent criticism.   Illness, loneliness, and the fogs of London drove him back to Paris, there to die on 17th October, 1849.   His grave is in Père Lachaise, close to Bellini's.   His heart is in Poland.

Chopin's Bequest

I know of no more futile occupation than an attempt to make a formal analysis of any work of Chopin, pointing out here the influence of Hummel or Weber, there his devotion to Bellini.   He was no orchestrator, and the two Concerti, with all their charming touches, are of secondary importance.   Apart from the three Sonatas, the most highly organised works are the four Ballades, for the 'programmes' of which the reader may be referred to M. Cortot's edition, and take with a grain of salt what that eminent pianist has to say about them.   The two books of Études remain unapproached for the unusual combination of technical virtuosity and sheer beauty: these alone make most subsequent writers for the piano appear as pygmies.   Brahms only is comparable, technically.   The *presto* Finale of the Sonata in B flat Minor, which has baffled so many commentators as being unorthodox and formless, stands to-day as one of the most astonishing pieces of impressionist writing in the whole literature of the piano.   The Nocturnes and Valses are unequal in merit, but include some that belong to that heritage which has survived a century of development and change.   The Slav element in Chopin would appear to be more subtly expressed in the Mazurkas than in anything else, and a proper estimate of their essence can, I feel, only be realised by those who have an intimate knowledge of the traditional folk-music of that part of Poland which gave inspiration to the composer.

It is possible that the low dynamic plane of Chopin's piano-playing may have been originally suggested to him by the technique of the clavichord.   In this connection it is worth noting the remarks of Hipkins, who knew Chopin well and heard him play many times when he was in England in 1848. (The remarks appear in a letter quoted by Miss A. M. Diehl in *Musical Memories*, 1897.)

His fortissimo was the pure full tone without noise, a harsh inelastic note being to him painful. His *nuances* were modifications of that tone, decreasing to the faintest yet always distinct pianissimo. His singing *legatissimo* touch was marvellous. The wide-extended arpeggios in the bass were transfused by touch and pedals into their corresponding sustained chords, and swelled or diminished like waves in an ocean of sound. He kept the elbows close to his side, and played only with finger-touch—no weight from the arms. He used a simple, natural position of the hands as conditioned by scale or chord-playing, adapting the easiest fingering—although it might be against the rules—that came to him. He changed fingers upon a key as often as an organ-player.

In our own day the tradition of Chopin-playing is probably best exemplified in the interpretations of Moritz Rosenthal (now a veteran of seventy-three) who was a pupil of Mikuli, who had studied with the composer himself. According to Rosenthal, the composer confined himself in his lessons strictly to the playing, and did not, like Liszt, dwell upon the music itself; he was always disinclined to discuss the merits or shortcomings of his own or other people's music. And it was *à propos* of pure technique that Chopin, in the last year of his life, wrote so whimsically: 'Nothing has come from my efforts except my long nose and my badly cultivated fourth finger.'

BIBLIOGRAPHY

BIDOU, HENRI: *Chopin.* (Paris, 1925.)

GANCHE, EDOUARD: *Frédéric Chopin; sa Vie et ses Œuvres.* (Paris, 1926.)

KARASOWSKI, MORITZ: *Life and Letters of Chopin.* Translated by E. HILL. Enlarged and Revised Edition. 12s. 6d. (Reeves, 1935.)

LUCAS, VERONICA: *Letters of George Sand*. 15s. (Routledge, 1930.)

MAINE, BASIL: *Chopin*. 2s. (Duckworth, 1933.)

MURDOCH, WILLIAM: *Chopin; his Life*. 16s. (Murray, 1934.)

NIECKS, FREDERICK: *The Life of Chopin*. 2 vols. 25s. (Novello, 1889.)

OPIENSKI, HENRY: *Chopin's Letters*. Translated by E. L VOYNICH. 18s. 6d. (Harmsworth, 1932.)

POURTALÈS, GUY DE: *Chopin ou le Poète*. (Paris, 1927.)

FRANZ LISZT

BORN 22 October 1811   DIED 31 July 1886

By Ralph Hill

Parents and Childhood

The Hungarian family of Liszt was probably of noble origin.
Their hall-mark was quantity as well as quality. Georg
Adam Liszt, born in 1755, married three times and was
responsible for twenty-six children. One of his elder sons,
Adam, entered the service of the famous Esterhazy family
at Eisenstadt; they were the patrons of Haydn, Hummel,
Cherubini and many other musicians. In 1810 Adam was
promoted land-steward on one of the Esterhazy estates at
Raiding, a small town near Vienna. He took this oppor-
tunity to get married to an Austrian girl named Anna Lager.
Near the end of the next year a son was born. He was
christened Franz.

Franz Liszt was brought up on music, for his father was a
keen amateur violinist, guitarist and pianist. At an early
age Franz was taught the rudiments of music and the elements of piano-playing. He showed such precocious gifts
that at nine he was considered good enough to play in public
Hummel's piano Concerto in E flat and to extemporise on
some popular melodies. Soon afterwards Adam arranged
a concert of his own at which Franz played a concerto by
Ries. He was next taken to Eisenstadt to show off his
prowess to Prince Esterhazy. The Prince was deeply impressed and a concert was arranged in his palace at Pressburg.
It was a huge success and a fund was at once subscribed to
enable Franz to undergo a proper musical training for six

years. Accordingly Adam gave up his post with the Esterhazy family and decided to devote himself entirely to his
son's interests. He went to see Hummel, who was Court
conductor at Weimar, but the distinguished composer and
pianist was not fond of prodigies and asked an impossible
fee for his services. The result was that Adam returned
home, packed up his belongings and moved to Vienna,
where he placed Franz under the care of Salieri for composition and of Czerny for piano. After a dozen lessons Czerny
was so pleased with the boy's progress that he insisted upon
teaching him for nothing.

The Beginning of a Brilliant Career

For two years Franz worked hard under Czerny, during
which time he became well known in Viennese society.
He played at various concerts in Vienna and Pesth. It is
said that Beethoven was present at one of the Vienna concerts, in 1823, and that, after Franz had played, Beethoven
mounted the platform, lifted up the little pianist and embraced
him.

Adam now considered that the time was ripe for the world
at large to know something of Franz, so father and son set
off on an extended concert tour through Germany, on to
Paris, and finally to London. While at Paris they visited
Cherubini, the august principal of the Conservatoire, in the
hope that Franz might be taken as his pupil. But Cherubini
politely pointed out that according to the regulations
foreigners could not be admitted to the Conservatoire. So
the next best thing, if Franz was to have a really wide and
thorough musical training, was to place him privately under
Reicha, the eminent theorist and scholar, and Paer, the
composer of numerous popular operas. Things went well,
for Franz's new masters were excellent. Furthermore,
important letters of introduction gained the young pianist
admittance to the houses of leading French families, and he

played at several special public concerts. *Le petit Litz* became the fashion and he was known as the 'ninth wonder of the world.'

In the summer of 1824 Franz and his father crossed the Channel and Franz made his London début at the Argyll Rooms and immediately created a sensation. A few days later at Drury Lane he 'consented to display his inimitable powers on the New Grand Piano Forte, invented by Sébastien Erard.' The programme included a Concerto by Hummel and an improvisation on a theme from 'The Barber of Seville.' Society was delighted, and he was invited to appear at a command performance before George IV. Franz remained in London till the new year, devoting his spare time to the composition of an opera in one act, 'Don Sancho,' that he had been commissioned in Paris to write. Having finished it, he returned to Paris to show it to Paer, who submitted it to the Académie Royale de Musique with a special recommendation. It was accepted and produced in the autumn at the Royal Opera House. A lengthy notice appeared in the London musical journal *The Harmonicon*, and although the libretto was severely handled the music was given the encouragement due to the youthful composer. In the overture, the writer says, 'many of the orchestral parts are treated with vigour and intelligence which would do honour to composers long disciplined to their art.' The opening paragraph of the notice is interesting, for it indicates the supremely high place Franz was already given as a pianist: 'The extraordinary youth, the composer of this opera, has just entered his thirteenth year. He has been acknowledged by some of the first connoisseurs of Germany and France to merit a place among the principal pianists of Europe; nay, some have gone so far as to say that he yields the palm to Hummel only, whose immense talent as an improvisatore undoubtedly stands as yet alone and unrivalled. But the youthful Liszt is also a composer and gifted with the talent of improvisation in a high degree.'

The next two years were spent in further tours in France and England. Then in 1827 Adam died and Franz was left to make shift for himself and look after his mother. On his death-bed Adam gave voice to an ominous warning. He told Franz that he had a good brain and a kind heart, but women would control and upset his life.

Before the last war a book was published in Germany entitled *Liszt und die Frauen*. The author recorded the details of some twenty-six *affaires des cœurs*.

First Love Affair

Liszt's mother now came to Paris to look after him. He threw himself body and soul into his work, practising and teaching some ten hours a day. As with most youths of a romantic and sensitive disposition two potent influences had begun to affect his whole attitude to life—religion and love; they were to dominate Liszt's whole outlook until he died. Among his pupils was a charming girl of sixteen, Caroline de Saint-Cricq, and needless to say—for Liszt was as striking in looks as he was in intelligence—pupil and master became infatuated with each other. Caroline's invalid mother encouraged their love-making, but soon she died and her husband, a Minister of the Interior, told Liszt that he had other plans for the future of his daughter. Liszt took his loss very badly and for months he remained in a state of nervous collapse. He never forgot Caroline: when he drew up his will in 1860 he left her a jewelled ring.

From childhood Liszt's favourite form of literature was the Bible, the lives of the Saints, and any other religious works he could procure. He dreamed himself 'incessantly into the world of saints,' and now he begged without avail to be allowed to enter the Paris seminary. 'I hoped,' he said, 'it might be granted me to live the life of the saints and perhaps die the death of the martyrs.'

During the following two years Liszt concentrated his

whole attention on perfecting his piano technique and reading with avidity theological works and romantic literature. In religion he turned to Lamennais and in politics to Saint-Simon. But 1830 was a decisive year in Liszt's life. He met Berlioz, Chopin, and Paganini, and became acquainted with their music; it was entirely in sympathy with his own romantic spirit and thus opened out a new world to him. The extraordinary virtuosity of Paganini was especially inspiring. Liszt felt that, since Paganini exploited to such artistic purpose new and wonderful effects on the violin, he could apply a similar technique to the piano. In addition, the delicate poetry and subtle sonorities of Chopin together with the brilliant and masterly orchestral achievements of Berlioz helped to nourish the seeds of his own style as a composer.

A year or two later Liszt writes to a friend: 'Here is a whole fortnight that my mind and fingers have been working like two lost spirits—Homer, the Bible, Plato, Locke, Byron, Hugo, Lamartine, Chateaubriand, Beethoven, Bach, Hummel, Mozart, Weber, are all around me. I study them, meditate on them, devour them with fury; besides this I practise from four to five hours of exercises (thirds, sixths, octaves, shakes, repeated notes, and cadenzas). Ah! provided I don't go mad, you will find an artist in me! Yes, an artist such as you desire, and such as is required nowadays!'

The True Romantic

During the first half of the nineteenth century Paris was the great centre of all the arts. Never had so much genius concentrated on one city. Among the great names were Chopin, Liszt, Berlioz, Meyerbeer, Rossini, Cherubini, Halévy, Auber, Ferdinand Hiller, Dumas, de Musset, George Sand, Victor Hugo, Balzac, Heine, Delacroix, Corot, Gautier, and a dozen others. Into this society of romantics Liszt flung himself. He absorbed much and became a worthy disciple of the new thought. When Liszt played in public his audience were swept off their feet with ecstasy, for not only did he play divinely but he acted superbly. Someone who was present at one of these musico-emotional orgies describes in his autobiography Liszt's playing of Mendelssohn's 'Lieder ohne Worte': 'As the closing strains began I saw Liszt's countenance assume that agony of expression, mingled with radiant smiles of joy, which I never saw in any other human face except in the paintings of Our Saviour by some of the early masters. His hands rushed over the keys, the floor on which I sat shook like a wire, and the whole audience were wrapped with sound, when the hand and the frame of the artist gave way. He fainted in the arms of a friend who was turning over the pages for him, and we bore him out in a strong fit of hysterics. The effect of the scene was really dreadful. The whole room sat breathless with fear, till Hiller came forward and announced that Liszt was already restored to consciousness and was comparatively well again.'

The year 1833 was conspicuous for two events of importance. Liszt completed the first of his great transcriptions —Berlioz's 'Symphonie Fantastique'—and met Countess d'Agoult, the first of the two women who dominated his life throughout. The Countess was twenty-eight years old, of high intelligence and romantic disposition; she possessed three children and a middle-aged husband with whom she had little in common. The result was that the striking young musical Spartan and the romantic young lady eloped. In her memoirs, written under the pen-name of 'Daniel Stern,' she speaks impersonally of their mutual attraction: 'Strong affinities of race and temperament brought them together, but the extreme differences in their education and their station in life of necessity raised up innumerable difficulties around them. A thousand obstacles arose between them and endowed the passion that drove them towards each other with a dolorous intensity which, in more balanced days than these, love will never again know.'

They went to Geneva and there was born a daughter, Blandine. That Dame Scandal should wag her tongue vigorously was to be expected, but the waggings became exceptionally vicious and frequent, since it was one thing for a Countess to take a lover from her own stratum of society, but quite another when he happened to be a mere musician. However, the happy couple were quite indifferent to the likes and dislikes of the venerable Dame. They had their friends—George Sand, for instance, who joined them at Chamonix where they all went picnicking in the mountain valleys, discussing the while art, philosophy, religion and the rest of the things that absorbed their interests.

A Musical Duel

On Liszt's return to Paris he found that his reputation as a pianist had been eclipsed by Thalberg, who had become the idol of musical society. Liszt gave a concert but sensed that his audience was not so responsive as before. He was piqued. Thalberg must be taught a lesson. Liszt's attitude towards his rival was not particularly admirable: he enjoyed hearing disparaging remarks about Thalberg and made no attempt to hide his own feelings. At last matters came to a head. Thalberg played at the Conservatoire before an audience of 400, while Liszt in opposition played at the Opera House before an audience of about ten times the number. Musical society took sides, and the general atmosphere was like that of an election. Finally, the two great pianists were engaged to appear together at the salon of a certain Princess. Liszt opened with his 'Niobe Fantasia' and Thalberg replied with his 'Moses Fantasia.' It was a battle of giants, and Liszt was unanimously proclaimed the victor. Sir Charles Hallé, who was in Paris at the time, has recorded his impressions of Liszt's virtuosity. 'Such marvels of executive skill and power,' he says, 'I could never have imagined. One of the transcendent merits of his playing was the crystal-like clearness which never failed for a moment, even in the most complicated and to anybody else impossible passages; it was as if he had photographed them in their minutest detail upon the ear of his listener.'

In 1837 Liszt and the Countess set off to Italy. At Como on 18th December their second daughter, Cosima, was born. In Milan Liszt renewed his friendship with Rossini, transcribed for piano the latter's 'William Tell' Overture and the group of songs entitled 'Les Soirées Musicales,' and played them in public. He also worked at a number of other transcriptions, the Paganini Études, and a few original compositions, some of which were later published as the second book of 'Années de Pèlerinage.' While in Venice, Liszt read of the terrible destruction caused by the Danube floods in Hungary. He immediately went alone—the Countess being indisposed—to Vienna and gave ten concerts that brought in nearly £2,000. He handed over the entire sum for the relief of his compatriots. Liszt returned to Venice and within a few days continued his travels with the Countess. During a short period in Rome a son, Daniel, was born.

Liszt had a dual personality. He was a strange mixture of a great and sincere artist, and a rather vulgar showman and actor: the one produced the glorious setting of the Thirteenth Psalm for baritone and orchestra, the B minor Piano Sonata, the 'Faust' and 'Dante' Symphonies, and the Fantasia and Fugue on B-A-C-H for organ, while the other turned out a profusion of pot-boilers of which the 'Hungarian Fantasia' is a fair specimen. One side of Liszt wanted a quiet life devoted to religious contemplation and to the service of music in its highest manifestations, but his other side craved for public applause and for the luxury and glitter of aristocratic drawing-rooms. He could be kind-hearted and callous, sincere and insincere, egotistical and modest by turns. In fact the man and artist were throughout an amazing contradiction.

It did not take long for the Countess to realise that her hero

was by no means the paragon of artistic and moral virtue
that she may have at first imagined. Liszt's visit to Vienna
opened her eyes rather more widely than was comfortable.
Despite the sacrifices she had made for him, and despite his
fondness for her, when he returned he prattled of nothing
else but his successes, particularly with the ladies, and of the
aristocrats with whom he had talked and dined. The
Countess tells us in her memoirs that 'he put out of sight the
compositions of his own that he had sketched. But he could
not so easily put them out of mind; and so, in his exasperation,
drawn as he was in opposite directions, he sought, in order
to escape from himself, distractions in the outer world,
whence I used to see him return more and more dissatisfied,
more and more out of equilibrium.'

In October 1839 the end of his *liaison* with the Countess
was in sight. They parted at Florence: Liszt to Vienna and
the Countess with the three children to Paris. In 1844 they
came to an understanding and separated for good. The
Countess turned to literature and some years later wrote a
novel entitled *Nélida* under her pen-name 'Daniel Stern.'
In reality this novel was a thinly disguised autobiography
with Liszt and herself as the chief characters. All Liszt's
failings are vividly and sometimes cruelly portrayed in the
character of Guermann, an artist. It is said that Liszt never
forgave the Countess. He did not even write to her when
their two children, Daniel and Blandine, died.

The Travelling Showman

From 1840 to 1848, now at the height of his powers as a
pianist, Liszt did nothing else but tour the length and breadth
of Europe revelling in a continuous orgy of hero-worship,
of which the like has never before or since been seen, except
perhaps for Paganini. He went to Hungary, Austria, England, Russia, Turkey, Poland, Denmark, Spain, Portugal,
Germany, and wherever it was he was received with regal

splendour. In Pesth two Counts and a Baron assisted by three slightly less distinguished nobles, all of them clad in gorgeous national costume, presented Liszt with a jewelled sabre; and after the ceremony he was accompanied to his hotel by a military band and a torch-light procession. In keeping with the romantic spirit of the times Liszt behaved and dressed in a most extravagant manner—green gloves and a different cravat for every day in the year were two items of dress that created an impression. Those who did not pay him the respect that he considered his due were made to feel the keen edge of his tongue. He even put Czar Nicholas I in his place for daring to talk while he was playing! On one of his tours Liszt took with him the notorious adventuress, Lola Montez, who was also much sought after by Ludwig I of Bavaria.

Although Liszt aroused great attention and enthusiasm in England, he was not treated with quite the same reverence that he enjoyed elsewhere. He certainly played at Buckingham Palace to the delight of Queen Victoria, but our aristocracy saw that he kept his place. His escapades on the barbarian Continent were common knowledge and therefore English gentlemen must be careful not to have their good names besmirched. Remember the Countess and her three illegitimate children . . . and it is said there have been others! A mere pianist too!

The Princess—Weimar

Suddenly Liszt's life as a travelling showman came to an end. Three things contributed to his beginning a new life. First, he was tiring of his superficial way of living, secondly, he met the woman who was to rule him during the rest of his days, and thirdly, he was offered the post of musical director of the Grand Ducal Court at Weimar.

In 1847 Liszt went to Kiev where he gave his last concerts. At one of them the Princess Carolyne von Sayn-Wittgenstein was present, and Liszt's wonderful playing and striking presence made a deep impression upon her. The Princess showed her pleasure by contributing handsomely to one of Liszt's charity concerts. He called on her and thanked her for her interest.

The result was to be expected.

The Princess was twenty-eight years of age. Born of Polish parents domiciled in Russia, she had inherited large estates at Kiev. At the age of seventeen she had been driven into marriage with a Russian prince by whom she had one child, a daughter. The marriage was a failure because Carolyne was a girl of considerable intellectual capacity. That Liszt was attracted by other qualities than physical beauty is fairly certain, judging from contemporary accounts of her plain and unattractive features. After all, she was an intelligent and wealthy princess, and Liszt adored titles and intelligent appreciation. Liszt went to stay with her at one of her estates. They read Dante, and Liszt decided to compose a 'Dante Symphony.'

Then came the Weimar period. The Princess established herself with Liszt at the Villa Altenburg, and hoped that a divorce could be speedily arranged. Unfortunately the Prince saw no reason why he should give up all his claims to his wife's wealth, so he clung to his legal bondage like grim death. What with turning night into day, smoking black cigars, and living in the same house as the Court musical director, the Princess was hardly considered an asset to Weimar by the good townsfolk.

One May day in 1849 Wagner, having found the Dresden police unsympathetic to his activities during the riots, presented himself at the Villa Altenburg. Liszt first met Wagner at Paris in 1840. In 1844 he heard 'Rienzi' at Dresden, where he again met Wagner four years later and had a long and intimate talk with him. Wagner stayed with Liszt at the Villa Altenburg for a week or two, but when the news came that the police were on his track again, it was thought expedient that Wagner should retreat to Paris. Meanwhile Liszt had begun to realise the extent of Wagner's immense genius, and from now onwards he put all his artistic influence and resources to the furtherance of Wagnerian ideals. Liszt produced 'Lohengrin' at Weimar in the following year. And his support did not end there: Liszt's purse was ever open to the demands of the impecunious Wagner.

George Eliot's Visit

During the next decade or so Weimar was turned into the centre of the 'new German school' and the Princess kept an open house, to which came a constant stream of distinguished people—philosophers, musicians, poets, painters, and novelists, including Thackeray and George Eliot. George Eliot records that 'Liszt looked splendid as he conducted the Opera. The grand outline of his face and floating hair was seen to advantage, as they were thrown into the dark relief by the stage lamps. Liszt's conversation is charming. I never met a person whose manner of telling a story was so piquant.' She went to breakfast at the Villa Altenburg and among the guests were Cornelius and Raff: 'The Princess was tastefully dressed in a morning robe of some semi-transparent material, lined with orange colour, which formed the bordering and ornament of the sleeves, a black lace jacket and a piquant cap on the summit of her comb, and trimmed with violet colour.' During a reading of poetry George Eliot sat next to Liszt and was carried away by 'the sweetness of his expression. Genius, benevolence, and tenderness beam from his whole countenance, and his manners were in perfect harmony with it. Then came the thing I had longed for—his playing. I sat near him so that I could see both his hands and face. For the first time in my life I beheld real inspiration—for the first time I heard the true tones of the piano. He played one of his compositions, one of a series of religious fantasies. There was nothing strange or excessive about his manner. His manipulation of the instrument was quiet and easy, and his face was simply grand—the lips compressed and the head thrown backward. When the music expressed quiet rapture or devotion a smile flitted over his features; when it was triumphant the nostrils dilated. There was nothing petty or egotistic to mar the picture.'

Liszt reorganised the Opera and conducted the Court concerts. In addition to the new works of contemporary composers, such as Wagner, Berlioz, Schumann, Raff and Cornelius, Liszt produced operas by Gluck, Mozart, Schubert, Donizetti, Meyerbeer, Spontini, Weber and a score of other great composers. His symphony concert programmes were no less wide in appeal: all the Beethoven symphonies including the practically unknown 'Choral,' Mozart, Haydn, Berlioz and so on. Liszt also displayed great activity as a composer. The 'Transcendental Études,' 'Hungarian Rhapsodies,' the twelve Symphonic Poems, and the 'Faust' and 'Dante' Symphonies all belong to this period.

Art before Politics

Although the world of music was divided into bitterly antagonistic parties fighting their battles under the banners of Mendelssohn, Schumann, and Wagner, no one could have been more level-headed and broad-minded than Liszt. His catholicity of taste was a form of genius. He could appreciate Wagner and Berlioz on the one hand and the Russian Nationalists on the other, while at the same time waxing enthusiastic over the merits of Mendelssohn, Schumann, and Chopin. And there was no question of shallow understanding. During this period of storm and stress that lasted throughout his life Liszt remained an untiring propagandist for, and an unbiased critic of, contemporary music: he was interested in everything that he considered good of its kind, no matter to what 'party' the composers might belong. Art came before politics. A composer himself, whose innovations were generally condemned as extravagances by the conservatives and the reactionaries and merely tolerated by the followers of the greater and even more spectacular genius of Wagner, Liszt was able to thrust aside any narrow prejudices that might have arisen against those who showed so little faith and interest in his own creative efforts. Had he been entirely self-centred, like most other great creative artists, no doubt his position as a composer would have been very different.

After Liszt and the Countess d'Agoult parted, it was decided that their three children should be placed in the care of Liszt's mother. All went well until the Princess gained control of Liszt. The Princess naturally disliked her predecessor and therefore it was not long before she prevailed upon Liszt to have the children brought up by her own former governess, an elderly lady with a rather sour disposition. Thus the Princess planned to have the children taken away from any possible influence of their real mother. Even their letters were censored and they were instructed to call the Princess 'mother.' Next to the Countess she considered Wagner the most pernicious influence in Liszt's life, and she did her best to poison Liszt against him, but she accomplished little in this direction. No doubt the Princess feared Wagner would not only outshine Liszt, but that the latter would eventually become indifferent to his own creative efforts.

Liszt's affairs went smoothly for the first half a dozen years, but at short notice the Princess was ordered to return to Russia. She refused and in consequence she was sentenced to banishment. The Grand Duchess of Saxe-Weimar, sister of the Czar, declined to have anything further to do with her and the rest of Weimar Society followed suit. At the same time Liszt was finding his position none too easy. First there were at his disposal only limited funds to carry out his artistic ideas, and secondly his colleague who was in charge of the Court drama pandered to the tastes of the Grand Duke and therefore pushed forward the claims of a more popular style of musical entertainment and his own department of drama. Finally in 1858 Liszt produced Cornelius's 'Barber of Bagdad,' and it was hissed. It was obvious that Liszt was really the target. Liszt at once decided that Weimar was best left to its own devices and he resigned forthwith.

The Princess and the Pope

Liszt and the Princess remained at Weimar until 1861. The Villa Altenburg was shut up and the Princess went to Rome to see if the Pope would grant the dissolution of her marriage. She threw herself at his feet and eloquently presented her case. The Pope was sympathetic and after due consideration agreed to her request. At last the Princess was free to marry Liszt. It was immediately arranged that Liszt should come to Rome on the eve of his fiftieth birthday and on the following day, 22nd October, they would be married at the church of San Carlo. But the Princess underestimated the power of the opposition, for at the eleventh hour, when all was ready for the ceremony, the Pope refused to allow the marriage to proceed. The Princess was in despair. Liszt certainly appears to have been upset, but in 1864, when the Prince died, no further talk of marriage was broached.

From now onwards the Princess concentrated all her energies upon religious speculation. For some time past she had been at work on a series of twenty-four huge tomes entitled *The Inner Causes of the Outer Weakness of the Church*. The more intense her spiritual and intellectual activities became, the more eccentric did she become in her mode of living. All day long and into the early hours of the morning, clad in fantastic colours, she sat cloistered in her study from which daylight and fresh air were carefully excluded. She puffed away at her black cigars continuously and the atmosphere was like that of a hot-house. Visitors, even Liszt himself, were obliged to wait in an ante-room for ten minutes in order to be 'de-ventilated' and rid of any fresh air that they might have brought in with them, before coming in contact with the Princess. 'That anyone survived,' says William Wallace in his fine study of *Liszt, Wagner, and the Princess*, 'after a mephitic whiff of the Princess's *salon* must be put down to an ever watchful Providence. Into this Paradise of Tainted Devices Liszt stepped day after day, and night after night.'

Liszt also turned to his religion. Ernest Newman in *The Man Liszt* gives a vivid picture of Liszt in his new environment. He 'tried to persuade himself that now he would give himself up heart and soul to his true vocation of solitary and saint. He settled down in a cloister that had been placed at his disposal in the church of Santa Maria del Rosario, on the Monte Mario. There was no one in the vast place but Liszt, a Dominican priest, and a servant. The priest read mass every morning; Liszt was always present, sitting in a stall a few yards from his cell. In the latter he had a long work-table, a small library, about a dozen pictures of saints, a marble cast of Chopin's hand, and a small piano of advanced age, badly out of tune, and with a D in the bass missing. But, as usual, he was making the best of two worlds. His tribute having been paid to the spirit in the morning, in the evening he let the flesh have its fling in the kind of company it loved. Shrewd observers were conscious of something suspiciously like a pose in his way of living.' In 1865, for some reason best known to himself, Liszt took minor orders and became an Abbé. He had already set about the task of reforming the music of the Church, with the result that a series of important works issued from his pen, such as 'The Legend of Saint Elizabeth' and 'Christus.'

Since giving up his post at Weimar, Liszt had lost his mother and his two children Blandine and Daniel. In 1857

Cosima had married Hans von Bülow, the famous pianist and conductor and a pupil of Liszt, but seven years later she left him to live with and devote herself to Wagner. Although such an action was true to family tradition, Liszt, who looked upon von Bülow almost as a son, could not countenance it, and consequently he became estranged from Wagner. It is characteristic of him, however, that he did not withdraw his ardent support of Wagner's cause, despite the fact that he was opposing the wishes of the Princess.

Rome, Weimar, and Pesth

From 1869 to 1886 Liszt divided his time between Rome, Weimar, where he had a large circle of pupils, and Pesth, where he directed the newly formed Hungarian Conservatoire. Nearly every pianist of note of the next generation studied at some time or other under Liszt. He refused all payment, demanding only that the student should have already acquired mastery of keyboard technique. Among those living to-day who were Liszt's pupils are Felix Weingartner, Frederic Lamond, Emil Sauer, and Moritz Rosenthal. Rosenthal says that Liszt was unique as a pianist: 'I remember when I first went to him as a boy—he was in Rome at the time—he used to play for me in the evening by the hour—nocturnes by Chopin, études of his own—all of a soft, dreamy nature that caused me to open my eyes in wonder at the marvellous delicacy and finish of his touch. The embellishments were like a cobweb—so fine—or like the texture of the costliest lace . . . Liszt was more wonderful than anybody I have ever known.'

Some time in 1873, Amy Fay, an American young lady, came to Weimar in the hope of studying under Liszt. On the day after her arrival she went to the theatre, where she saw Liszt in a box. Her first impressions of the great man are interesting: 'Liszt is the most interesting and striking-looking man imaginable. Tall and slight, with deep-set eyes, shaggy eye-brows, and long iron-grey hair, which he wears parted in the middle. His mouth turns up in the corners, which gives him a most crafty and Mephistophelian expression when he smiles, and his whole appearance and manner have a sort of Jesuitical elegance and ease. His hands are very narrow, with long and slender fingers that look as if they had twice as many joints as other people's! They are so flexible and supple that it makes you nervous to look at them. Anything like the polish of his manner I never saw. When he got up to leave the box, for instance, after his adieu to the ladies, he laid his hand on his heart and made his final bow—not with affectation, or in mere gallantry, but with a quiet courtliness which made you feel that no other way of bowing to a lady was right or proper. It was most characteristic. But the most extraordinary thing about Liszt is his wonderful variety of expression and play of feature. One moment his face will look dreamy, shadowy, tragic. The next he will be insinuating, amiable, ironic, sardonic; but always the same captivating grace of manner. He is a perfect study. I cannot imagine how he must look when he is playing. He is all spirit, but half the time, at least, a mocking spirit, I should say. All Weimar adores him, and people say that women still go perfectly crazy over him. When he walks out he bows to everybody just like a King!'

Crazy Women

That women still went crazy over Liszt was no matter of idle talk. He was nearly shot by one admirer, and another stripped the covering off a chair on which he had been sitting and hung it on the wall in a frame. Others would surround him while he played and pluck out his hairs with special tweezers! Perhaps the most incredible story, not to say the most revolting, is that of an elderly lady who neither smoked nor took snuff and, although fastidious over matters of personal cleanliness, exhaled a curious and obnoxious odour. It was discovered that in 1843, after a public dinner, she had obtained the stump of Liszt's cigar, which she placed in her corsage, where it remained for over twenty-five years!

In 1872 Liszt had a reconciliation with Wagner and, contrary to the wishes of the Princess, took part in the ceremony of laying the foundation-stone of the Bayreuth Theatre. In the following year the Hungarians organised a national celebration in honour of Liszt's fiftieth anniversary as a concert pianist. Three years later the Countess d'Agoult died, but Liszt appears to have been unmoved by the news. In 1876 Liszt attended the first Bayreuth Festival and in 1882 was present at the first performance of 'Parsifal,' after which he spent several weeks with Wagner in Venice. He returned to Pesth and on February 13th, 1883, learned of Wagner's death. His grief was heightened by the fact that Cosima requested that he should not come to the funeral. The next year he went to the Bayreuth Festival, but Cosima was too busy to see him.

Last Tour and Death

In 1886 Liszt went on his last tour. First to Paris where his 'Gran Mass' was performed under Colonne, and then to London for the first time after forty-five years. Here he spent two weeks, staying at Sydenham with Mr. and Mrs. Littleton. Sir Alexander Mackenzie conducted the 'Legend of St. Elizabeth' and Liszt visited Windsor Castle where he played once again to Queen Victoria. He continued his tour on to Antwerp, Brussels, Paris, Weimar, Bayreuth, and Luxemburg. On his way to Bayreuth to attend the Festival in July, Liszt was obliged to pass a night in the train. He caught a chill and on arriving at Bayreuth spent the day in bed. Against the doctor's orders he attended the performance of 'Tristan und Isolda,' but after the death scene of Isolda he was forced to leave. Pneumonia set in and the doctor foolishly refused to allow him to have his brandy, of which he was used to drinking a bottle a day. Congestion of the lungs followed, he became delirious, and on Saturday night, July 31st, Liszt died. Two hours previously he had spoken his last word. It was 'Tristan.'

And what of the Princess? On learning the news of Liszt's death she shut herself up completely, refusing to see or write to anyone. Towards the end of February the following year she completed the twenty-fourth volume of her *magnum opus*. Within a fortnight she was found dead in bed.

BIBLIOGRAPHY

CORDER, FREDERICK: *Liszt*. 3s. 6d. (Kegan Paul, 'Masters of Music' Series, 1925.)

HERVEY, ARTHUR: *Franz Liszt*. 4s. 6d. (Lane, 1911.)

HILL, RALPH: *Liszt*. 2s. 6d. (Duckworth, 'Great Lives' Series, 1939.)

MACKENZIE, ALEXANDER: *Liszt*. 1s. 6d. (Murdoch, 'Mayfair Biographies,' 1922.)

NEWMAN, ERNEST: *The Man Liszt*. 12s. 6d. (Cassell, 1934.)

SITWELL, SACHEVERELL: *Liszt*. 15s. (Faber, 1934.)

JACOB LUDWIG FELIX
MENDELSSOHN-BARTHOLDY

BORN 3 February 1809   DIED 4 November 1847,

By Max Pirani

Descent

The life of Felix Mendelssohn-Bartholdy, examined in the
light of his ancestry, presents an interesting example of a
development that proceeded not by reversion to type, but
by means of a contrasting evolution.

He was born in Hamburg, of Jewish parents with Jewish
traditions rooted in Jewish culture, but though one can find
in his spiritual internationalism, his restlessness, his 'Wander-
lust,' and in the fluidity and adaptability of his genius, that
residuum of his Jewish ancestry which has enriched European
music with a glow of Oriental colour, yet nowhere in his work
çan be discovered even a trace of either the Synagogue or the
traditional lamentations which such an origin would suggest.

Indeed, his artistic heritage was the purely Teutonic and
Christian music of his adored Bach and of Handel, his
intellectual upbringing was based on German and international literature, and his life was spent in an almost exclusively non-Jewish social *milieu*.

It was Felix's grandfather who accomplished the emergence
from the Ghetto, a feat of considerable difficulty, requiring
strength of character combined with unusual intellectual
capacity, but Moses Mendelssohn's qualities went beyond
these limits, for he became a master of German philosophy
and his research paved the way to much original work in
metaphysics and æsthetics.

His sons were brought up in an enlightened atmosphere; so much did Moses's religious breadth of view permeate his family that a break with the Jewish faith resulted. His second son, Abraham, and his two daughters became converts to Christianity, but before Abraham took this step his children, among them Felix, had been baptised.

Abraham had married Lea Salomon, a Jewess of Berlin, and it was on the advice and example of Lea's brother that the conversion was decided. The name of Bartholdy, then adopted, was due to the same influence, for it had been that of the former owner of Salomon's garden!

Youth

When Felix was three years old, his family escaped to Berlin, for life in Hamburg had become complicated by the French occupation. Abraham was a banker and, foreign domination proving as detrimental to his business as it was distasteful to his feelings, Berlin offered better prospects and a freer life.

Lea was a highly cultured woman and an excellent musician, and Felix and his sister Fanny had every encouragement to develop their abilities. Musical education began with five minute lessons and Felix's progress was not forced; before long it was he who set the pace, leaving his mother and his sister to admire his precocity.

At the age of seven he was taken to Paris where he was taught the piano by Madame Bigot and for the first time was influenced from outside the family circle.

On the return to Berlin his education, musical and otherwise, began in earnest. He studied piano with Ludwig Berger, musical theory with Zelter (who was Goethe's musical oracle), and languages with Heyse (the father of Paul Heyse the novelist); he also learned to draw and to play the violin.

At the age of nine he played in public for the first time and 'was much applauded.' At the age of twelve he began to compose systematically and prolifically, and from this time onwards his future career as a musician was accepted as a matter of course.

His environment was conducive to an easy and harmonious development of his talents. The Mendelssohn household was in the habit of having frequent musical evenings, at which the four children, Felix, Fanny, Rebecka, the younger sister, and Paul, performed. Felix's compositions were often included in the programmes and he had invaluable opportunities of playing and conducting before an audience. Abraham's position as a successful business man and Lea's artistic gifts had been instrumental in creating a *salon*, which many Berlin notabilities attended regularly and which attracted most visiting musicians.

Among the latter was Weber, who came to Berlin in 1821. He cast the same spell upon Felix as he did later upon Wagner and the enthusiasm he aroused remained with Felix throughout his life. Another contact of the same year was with Goethe, when Zelter took Felix to Weimar and introduced him to the poet. The boy's mentality can be gauged by this letter written to his parents describing the visit:

'*November 6th*, 1821.

'After church I went to the Elephant Hotel where I made a sketch of Lucas Cranach's house. Two hours later Professor Zelter came, calling out: "Goethe has come, the old gentleman has come!" We instantly hurried downstairs and went to Goethe's house. He is very kind but I do not think any of his portraits are like him. . . .

'After that I walked in the garden with him and Professor Zelter. He does not look like a man of seventy-three, rather of fifty. . . .

'Every morning I get a kiss from the author of *Faust* and *Werther*, and every afternoon two kisses from the father and friend Goethe. Think of that! In the afternoon I play to Goethe for about two hours, partly Bach fugues and partly improvisations.'

Another journey that left lasting impressions was a family tour of Switzerland in 1822 and for the first time Felix's composition reacted to the influence of national idiom, to be developed later in such works as the Scotch and Italian Symphonies: not that the pieces founded on Swiss tunes dating from this period have any great artistic significance, but they betray a readiness to assimilate external ideas that proved to be of great importance in Felix's development as a composer.

A similar influence was the outcome of a visit to the Baltic in 1824 when Felix first saw the sea, but this time the period of gestation was longer, and it is in the overture 'Meeresstille,' composed four years later, that these impressions were translated into sound.

Moscheles was a visitor to Berlin in the same year and spent much time with the Mendelssohns. He gave Felix piano lessons, though by this time the boy had become, in Moscheles's own words, a mature artist, and had attained more than local celebrity.

In Paris in 1825 he appeared both as pianist and composer. He seems to have made a better impression on the French musicians than they made on him, for in his letters he complains of ignorance, of charlatanism and of irreverence in the performance of great music.

Abraham's business was flourishing, and in 1825 he bought a new house, the family home of the future. His resources, pecuniary and social, were always at the disposal of Felix, who was spared many of those struggles so often associated with artistic achievement. Abraham in his paternal pride said wittily, 'Formerly I was the son of my father, now I am the father of my son'; an instance of commerce bowing to the arts in the true Jewish tradition. The racial heritage was also reflected in family attachments, especially in that of Felix and Fanny, a relationship intensified by similarity of taste and temperament.

Shakespeare and Bach

In 1826 Felix and Fanny read some of Shakespeare's plays and the immediate result was the composition of the Overture to *A Midsummer Night's Dream*. This, written for piano duet before it was orchestrated, demonstrated the principle of placing design before colour, a principle followed by Felix constantly both in his own method of composition and in the theories he propounded in his later teaching days.

His only noteworthy achievement in opera dates from this same period. 'Die Hochzeit des Camacho' had been written a year earlier, but in the negotiations for its performance in 1827 Felix met with the first serious obstructions of his career: he overcame them finally, though Spontini, then Director of the Berlin Opera, put every obstacle in the way both of the rehearsals and of the performances. The work was adversely criticised in the Press and by the public, and partly for this reason and also because he never again found a libretto to his liking, it was his last effort in the operatic form.

This creative activity did not retard his general cultural development and his matriculation at the Berlin University followed studies in literature and classical philology. His recreations included gymnastics, swimming, dancing, billiards and chess; and neither now, nor when his professional career grew more arduous, did he allow these diversions to be excluded from his life.

Felix, from early youth, had been a fanatical lover of Bach's music, an inheritance from Lea. Her remark when Fanny was a baby, four years before Felix was born, that 'the child has Bach fugue fingers,' indicated the tastes that were to be inculcated in her children. Bach's works were little known in Germany at this time and Felix, in his determination to share his own joys with the world, prepared a revival of the 'St. Matthew Passion.' The preparations began with the organisation of a small choir for private rehearsal and culminated in a public performance on 11th

March, 1829, the first since the death of Bach. There was great opposition to the project (even Zelter at first lacked confidence in the practicability of a performance) but Felix, together with a few fellow enthusiasts, including Devrient, a well-known singer, actor and littérateur, succeeded in carrying out the plan. So much public interest was aroused that the work was repeated on Bach's birthday, 21st March.

This successful outcome of Felix's altruistic efforts had far-reaching results: it was the beginning of the movement that led to the formation of the Bach Gesellschaft; it inaugurated, by the creation of interest amongst a public to whom the composer had been literally unknown, the Bach-cult of our own day; and it caused Felix to allude to his ancestry. 'It was an actor and a Jew,' he said to Devrient, 'who restored this great Christian work to the people.'

Travel

Felix's musical career up to the age of twenty had been meteoric but profitless, and it was now decided that he should prepare to live by his profession. Berlin had become uncomfortable, for his fellow musicians were antagonistic, partly because of his youthful egotism and partly on account of his racial origin, which no amount of holy water could conceal. His black hair with its natural wave emphasised the Jewish features, and Thackeray in describing him ('His face is the most beautiful I ever saw, like what I imagine our Saviour's to have been') was not making Italian Primitives the basis of his comparison.

So foreign travel was ordained to combine a professional career with observation and experience of the world at large. There was even a suggestion that Felix's permanent home might be found outside his own country, and in the search for a possible future field of activity, he visited London in 1829. This, the first of ten visits that he paid to England, proved a momentous experiment. He appeared as composer, conductor and pianist with equal success in each role. His charming manner was a great asset and he danced, dined and was fêted to such an extent that his father wrote admonishing him not to forsake music for Society. He renewed acquaintance with Moscheles and made many friendships which were to stand him in good stead in later life.

At the end of the London musical season he went to Scotland, where natural beauties gave him inspiration for the 'Fingal's Cave' Overture; the thematic material of the Scotch Symphony can also be traced to this period. On the return to London in September, an accident—he fell from a carriage—kept him in bed for two months and prevented his attendance at Fanny's wedding: she married Wilhelm Hensel, the painter, in October.

Felix reached Berlin to find that a Chair of Music had been founded at the Berlin University with himself as the proposed occupant, but he was not ready to embrace a pedagogic career and declined the honour in favour of continuing his journeyings.

Through Weimar, Munich and Vienna (where he writes in disgust of the prevalent musical taste) he went to Italy, arriving in Rome in November, 1830. The following winter was devoted mainly to the assimilation of impressions, musical and artistic, and his numerous and detailed letters give a vivid picture of his experiences. He was enthusiastic about the singing of the Papal Choir in Palestrina and Allegri, but the ritual music of the Catholic Church, especially the chanting of the Psalms, was too much for a Lutheran upbringing superimposed on a Jewish mentality, and he neither understood nor liked it

His travels next took him through Switzerland, where he walked over mountain passes, sketched, wrote lengthy descriptive letters, and played the organ at remote churches. By way of Munich and Düsseldorf (a visit that was to have an important sequel) he found his way to Paris, where the most noteworthy meetings were with Chopin and Liszt.

He had by this time decided to settle in Germany, but before returning home he once more visited England. This time his organ-playing, particularly a performance at St. Paul's Cathedral, attracted great attention. He may be said to have brought to this country a new technique, especially in the treatment of the pedals, which was to become the basis of English organ-playing.

He returned to Berlin in July, 1832, and at the instance of Devrient applied for the post of Director of the Singakademie, vacant on account of Zelter's death. Perhaps Felix's refusal of the University professorship two years earlier had repercussions during the election that followed his application, or perhaps the earlier prejudices were still strong; in any case the candidature was a failure and he lost by a wide margin of votes. Berlin was not yet his, but he ignored defeat, and gave several concerts during the ensuing winter, introducing to Berlin, besides new works of his own, Beethoven's Pianoforte Concerto in G.

Düsseldorf

The year 1833 marked a turning-point in Felix's life: hitherto he had been a musical free-lance, but now he was offered a definite appointment. This followed on his conductorship of the Lower Rhine Festival. The offer was a contract for a period of three years, during which he was to direct the Opera, the theatre, and all other public musical establishments of Düsseldorf.

But Düsseldorf was too conservative to hold him: the new broom swept too clean. Felix began by dismissing the Director of Church Music, and performed Palestrina Masses instead of the customary insipidities. Then he attacked the Opera to such purpose that at the first performance under his directorship there was a riot in the audience. A lack of business instinct was partly responsible for his troubles, and he over-estimated both the Düsseldorfers' capacity for artistic appreciation and the prices they were prepared to pay for their seats.

After a few difficult months he asked to be released from the main part of his duties, retaining only the position of Honorary Intendant. However, he remained resident in Düsseldorf for more than a year longer, composing a great deal and conducting there and elsewhere, but the preliminary arrangements for the opening of a new theatre led to so much discord and such mental distress on Felix's part that, on being invited to become conductor of the Leipzig Gewandhaus Concerts, he made haste to accept, and moved to Leipzig in October, 1835.

Leipzig

Felix afterwards wrote, 'When I first came to Leipzig, I thought I was in Paradise,' and indeed Purgatory seemed to have been left behind, for his new appointment was highly congenial. Ferdinand David was his Konzertmeister (this brilliant violinist was born in Hamburg, in the same house as Felix) and they worked together in amity and in complete sympathy: the Violin Concerto was a later outcome of the friendship. The business management of the concerts was not Felix's duty and he could again devote his energies exclusively to music.

One of the first visitors was Chopin, to whom Felix introduced Clara Wieck: she and Schumann had made Felix's acquaintance soon after his arrival in Leipzig. Moscheles came immediately afterwards and he, Clara and Felix played Bach's Triple Concerto in D minor at one of the first concerts of the new regime.

On Moscheles's departure, Felix paid a flying visit with him to Berlin and for the last time saw Abraham, who died suddenly just after the return to Leipzig. This was the first break in the family circle and it affected Felix very deeply. He went so far as to write 'a new life must now begin for me, or all must be at an end—the old life is severed.' But the immediate result was to stimulate his work on the oratorio 'St. Paul,' begun in Düsseldorf, and in which Abraham had taken great interest. Together with his enthusiasm for the Leipzig concerts, this occupation prevented his loss from becoming an obsession.

Notable performances of Beethoven's Choral Symphony and Mozart's D minor Pianoforte Concerto were among the events of the first Gewandhaus season, Felix appearing both as conductor and pianist. His reputation as the latter had not diminished and contemporary criticism gives him a high place as a virtuoso.

The first performance of 'St. Paul' had been arranged to take place in Frankfurt, but the illness of Schelbe, the Director of the Frankfurt Cäcilien-Verein, necessitated its transference to the Lower Rhine Festival at Düsseldorf. However, Felix was destined to visit Frankfurt without delay, and the opportunity came when he was asked to take over Schelbe's duties on the termination of the Leipzig season.

In Frankfurt he fell in love, and this new experience had a devastating effect: he wrote, 'I can neither compose, nor write letters, nor play the piano!' The cause of this emotional upheaval was Mademoiselle Cécile Jeanrenaud, the daughter of a clergyman of the French Reformed Church, who, fortunately for 'Elijah' and other unwritten works, reciprocated his feelings. Their marriage took place in March, 1837, after a winter almost devoid of composition, though a strenuous season in Leipzig could not be avoided.

On his marriage, Felix finally cast aside all hereditary inhibitions: he was now a Christian gentleman and Berlin and London were to recognise him as such. Leipzig University had already conferred upon him the honorary degree of Ph.D., and his importance as a leading figure in musical life was continually increasing.

The Birmingham Festival brought him to England again in the autumn of 1837. He conducted 'St. Paul,' played his new Pianoforte Concerto (in D minor) and gave an organ recital. His propaganda for Bach continued in frequent performances of the great organ works, and he is reported to have aroused intense enthusiasm by his unconventional and grandiose interpretations.

Through Frankfurt, where he had left Cécile, he returned to Leipzig. The Gewandhaus concerts were resumed, and Felix introduced new features into the programmes. Historical and international grouping of composers was intended to acquaint his audience with the development of music, while new works, including many of his own, were frequently performed.

His first son was born on 7th February, 1838, and was christened Carl Wolfgang Paul: each of his five children was to be provided with three names, perhaps on account of his own richness in this respect. Cécile had a serious illness after the confinement, and for Felix this was the first of several periods of anxiety caused by family ill-health.

After a visit to Berlin, which had as its object the introduction of Cécile to Lea and Fanny, Felix began to sketch the preliminaries for 'Elijah.' He had decided on this after flirting with the idea of an oratorio on the subject of 'St. Peter,' but the Old Testament prophet proved the stronger attraction. The composition was to occupy Felix for nearly eight years.

In 1840 Liszt played in Leipzig, and created a bad impression by charging exorbitant prices. Felix arranged a musical soirée for him at the Gewandhaus, in order to pacify both the virtuoso and his public, providing thereby an instance of the friendly attitude he held towards his colleagues.

New Projects

Felix's popularity with the Saxon Government encouraged him to propose the establishment of a Conservatorium of

Music in Leipzig. The funds were to be provided by a legacy which had been bequeathed to the town, and Felix considered that an opportune moment had arrived to strike in the cause of Art. From 1840 to 1843 negotiations were in progress: Felix had lost the impatience of the Düsseldorf days and was prepared to work steadily towards the fulfilment of his desires. He also initiated a scheme to erect a monument to Bach in front of the Thomas-Schule, and he gave concerts and recitals in order to raise the necessary funds.

The 'Lobgesang,' composed as a *pièce d'occasion*, was the reason for his next English visit (the sixth), for the work was to be performed at the 1840 Birmingham Festival and Felix was invited to conduct it; this time he was in England only a few days. The 'Lobgesang' was given twice in Leipzig during the following season and its favourable reception, including expressions of enthusiasm from the King of Saxony, raised hopes for the prospects of the Conservatorium.

But trouble was brewing for Felix, and ambitions for Leipzig were to remain in the background for some time yet. His brother Paul came to visit him with a proposal, confirmed officially later, that he, Felix, should take charge of the Music Department of an Academy of Arts, to be founded in Berlin at the instance of Wilhelm IV, the new King of Prussia.

Felix foresaw difficulties, and in any case a change from the contented, productive life in Leipzig was not attractive, but the nature of the invitation, which gradually assumed the shape of a Royal Command, left the reluctant subject without choice, and after a busy winter in Leipzig, that concluded with a performance of Bach's Passion in St. Thomas's Church, he removed to the family house in Berlin in May, 1841.

His fears were well founded: ignorance and intrigue hampered his activities. As Kapellmeister to the King of Prussia he had theoretically a free hand, but he found himself involved in a series of conferences that produced no results. He wrote in October, after five months of abortive effort, 'If you allude to the project for establishing a Music Conservatorium here (in Berlin), then I regret to be obliged to say that I know no more about it than everyone else. . . . Years may pass, nothing may ever come of it.'

This discouragement was intensified by dissensions in the orchestra under his charge, and by the coldness of the public. At the King's request, he wrote music to the *Antigone* of Sophocles and, as usual, found in composition an escape from mundane vexations. The completion of the Scotch Symphony was an excuse for him to leave Berlin for its first Leipzig performance in March, 1842, and again for its first London performance at a Philharmonic concert in June. This time Cécile accompanied him across the Channel and was a witness of his popularity in England.

Felix received two Commands to Buckingham Palace, and he recounts with some naïveté his reception by Queen Victoria and the Prince Consort, the account commencing, 'Yesterday evening I was sent for by the Queen, who was almost (!) alone with Prince Albert.' He played the piano to the royal couple, heard the Prince Consort play the organ, and heard the Queen sing. The only blot on this golden page was provided by the royal parrot, which drowned the music with its screams, so that Felix had to carry it out of the room, cage and all.

Felix delayed his return to Berlin as long as possible, touring Switzerland in the summer, visiting Frankfurt in September, and stopping at Leipzig to conduct the first Gewandhaus concert of the season. In Berlin he found the organisation of the Academy as far from completion as ever and, losing patience, he tendered his resignation. This was accepted in part, but he yielded to the King of Prussia's persuasion that his appointment should merely be modified. He was now to be 'General Music Director,' certain compositions were demanded from him, he had special responsibilities concerning church music, but, for the present, he was not obliged to reside in Berlin.

He at once moved to his beloved Leipzig, but was hardly settled there when Lea died, an event which caused him great grief, particularly as his leaving Berlin had affected her severely.   But once again he found relief in his work, which was soon resumed with the old vigour.

The Conservatorium

The King of Saxony had at last agreed to Felix's plans for the Leipzig Conservatorium and in April, 1843, it was opened in the Gewandhaus buildings. The staff of professors included himself, Schumann and David. Felix supervised the whole of the teaching, and also gave individual piano lessons.   His instruction was confined to the interpretative aspect; he left technical routine to be dealt with by assistants, a method hardly consistent with modern ideas!

The King of Prussia was asking for the compositions he had commissioned, and the first of these to be finished was the 'Incidental Music to *A Midsummer Night's Dream.*'   The first performance was given in Berlin in October and, in view of the increasing pressure of work arising from the King's demands, Felix decided that he must again move his household.   Since his mother's death, the family house was his property and in November he was once more installed there.

Arrangements had been made for Ferdinand Hiller to conduct the Leipzig concerts, for Felix was overworking, and overworried: the Berlin annoyances, the constant journeys, and the ever-present thoughts of 'Elijah' were proving a strain on his strength, but he could not rest and accepted an offer from the Philharmonic Society of London to conduct six concerts in the summer of 1844.

The Conservatorium was in the meantime feeling its way without the services of its Director, but it had been judiciously organised and Felix, knowing that there was no fear of its extinction, was content to leave it until his energies could again be devoted freely to professional duties.

After a short stay in Frankfurt, he made one more attempt to solve the Berlin problems, but without success, and again he resigned all those duties that required him to reside in the capital. This time the King of Prussia acquiesced, and in December, 1844, Felix took the only course consistent with his physical condition, going back to Frankfurt for a long holiday.

It was not until the following September that he was fit to resume active work, though he had been composing consistently throughout the year. The attractions of the Conservatorium and the Gewandhaus Orchestra proved too strong to be disregarded indefinitely and he returned to Leipzig as soon as his health would permit.

During the winter of 1845–6 Felix worked at high pressure. He taught pianoforte and composition at the Conservatorium, conducted the Gewandhaus concerts and concentrated intensely on 'Elijah.' One act of importance to Leipzig was the invitation he sent to Moscheles to become pianoforte professor at the Conservatorium: it was accepted, and Moscheles proved invaluable to the institution when Felix was forced finally to cease work.

'Elijah'

Whether or not 'Elijah' can be ranked as highly as the productions of Felix's youth, it nevertheless marks the culmination of his career as a composer. Throughout the past eight years of triumphs and discouragements, the oratorio had been constantly in his mind: he spared no pains to make it, from both the technical and the musical aspects, as perfect a work as he was capable of conceiving. He gave his whole heart to its composition and taxed his strength to a degree that was evident only when the work was completed. He had the satisfaction of witnessing its success, but even this meant added effort, and his last two visits to England at a time when he should have been conserving his energies hastened the final breakdown.

He made other journeys before these: in May and June, 1846, three weeks were spent travelling in the Rhineland, where he conducted successively at Aix, Düsseldorf, Liège, and Cologne. He had success everywhere, but returned to Leipzig tired, faced with the task of completing 'Elijah' in time for the Birmingham Festival.

After rehearsals in London, Felix conducted the first performance of 'Elijah' in Birmingham Town Hall on 26th August. It met with overwhelming enthusiasm, and Felix himself wrote equally enthusiastically of its performance and of the audience's reception. The journey home fatigued him greatly, but he immediately began the final revision of the oratorio of which almost every movement was altered before publication.

He was overtaxing himself constantly: a demand from the King of Prussia for a setting of the German Liturgy set him to further composition and this work, together with some others, was written during a short creative burst. Moscheles had arrived and had taken over the direction of the Conservatorium: Niels Gade had relieved him of the main part of his conductor's duties; but Felix insisted on taking charge of some of the Gewandhaus concerts and on instituting examinations of students in his capacity of Conservatorium Director.

He even began work on another oratorio, to be called 'Christus,' and by the time he left Leipzig in April, 1847, for the London performance of 'Elijah,' his appearance reflected his exhausted state. He spent a busy month in England, conducting 'Elijah' four times in London and once each in Manchester and Birmingham, conducting and playing at a Philharmonic concert, giving pianoforte and organ recitals, and again visiting Buckingham Palace.

He returned to Frankfurt in September, weary and ill, and two days after his arrival heard of Fanny's death. This had a disastrous effect: it was a blow from which he never recovered. Switzerland welcomed him again in early summer, but he could not work, and spent his time drawing and painting. In September he returned home to Leipzig and found commissions waiting for him, but he refused them all: a string quartet and a few fragments were all that was written in these last months.

A visit to Berlin was too vivid a reminder of Fanny and further reduced his condition. Fits of depression were followed by a serious attack of shivering and head pains on 9th October: after a temporary recovery he relapsed, and from a third attack on 3rd November he never recovered consciousness. He died on 4th November.

Mendelssohn's epitaph could hardly be better expressed than in the words of Dr. H. C. Colles, who writes in Grove's *Dictionary*, 'he was the composer whose versatile abilities dominated the musical taste of Germany during his life, and of England for a generation or more after his death.'

BIBLIOGRAPHY

HENSEL, S.: *The Mendelssohn Family*. O.P. (Low, 1880.)

MOSCHELES, FELIX: *The Letters of Felix Mendelssohn*. O.P. (Trübner, 1888.)

ROCKSTRO, W. S.: *Mendelssohn*. O.P. (Low, 1900.)

STRATTON, S. S.: *Mendelssohn*. 5s. 6d. (Dent, 'The Master Musicians' Series, 1934.)

MODESTE PETROVICH MOUSSORGSKY

BORN 21 March 1839   DIED 28 March 1881

By M. D. Calvocoressi

Origins and Early Childhood

Modeste Petrovich Moussorgsky was born in the village of Karevo in the Pskov Government, the son of a well-to-do landowner. The family harked back to a certain Roman Vassilievich Monastyrev (himself a descendant of a Prince Smolensky, of the lineage of Rurik), who lived in the fifteenth century and bore the nickname Moussorga—said to have meant 'the slanderer,' or backbiter. The composer's grandfather, an officer of the Imperial Guards, had married one of his serfs, Irene Yegorova, who bore him three daughters and a son, Peter. The resulting strain of peasant blood may help to account for the strong instinct which was to drive Modeste to study and depict the humble people, and for his intimate comprehension of their minds and souls.

Peter married Julia Chirikova, belonging, like himself, to the landed gentry. They had four sons, two of whom died in childhood, the other two being Philaret (born 1836) and Modeste. Practically nothing is known of Peter Moussorgsky except that, according to Modeste's autobiography (of which more anon), he worshipped music. And all we know of his wife is that she was of a romantic disposition, fond of writing verse, but not endowed with any poetic talent, and that she played the piano.

There is the same scarcity of reliable information as to

Modeste's childhood and boyhood. In fact, all that we know is contained in his autobiography, which he wrote in 1880, a few months before his death. This informs us that, 'under the influence of his nurse, he became familiar with the old Russian tales. It was mainly his familiarity with the very spirit of the life of the people that impelled him to extemporise music before knowing even the most elementary rules of piano-playing. His mother gave him his first piano lessons.

'When at the piano, he hated having to do as he was told. Nevertheless he made such progress that at the age of seven he was able to play small pieces by Liszt; and at a party in his parents' home, at the age of eleven, he performed, in front of a large audience, a big concerto by Field. His father, who worshipped music, decided to develop his ability, and his musical education was carried on under Herke at Petersburg. This teacher was so pleased with his pupil that he made him play, at the age of twelve, a concert rondo by Hertz at a charity affair given at the house of Mrs. Riumin, a lady-in-waiting. The success and the impression created by the young musician's playing was so great that Herke, although an exacting taskmaster, presented him with a copy of Beethoven's Sonata in A flat major.

'At thirteen, young Moussorgsky entered the school of the cadets of the Guards. At that time he composed a small piano piece which he inscribed to his comrades. It was his first published composition. At the school he sought the company of Father Kroupsky, the religious instructor, and succeeded, thanks to him, in acquiring a deep knowledge of the very essence of old church music, Greek and Catholic. At the age of seventeen, he entered the Preobrajensky Regiment. One of his brother officers introduced him to the great composer Dargomyjsky, at whose house Moussorgsky became acquainted with the leading representatives of musical art in Russia, Cesar Cui and M. Balakirev. With the latter the nineteen-year-old composer studied the whole history of the evolution of musical art, by means of actual examples, with systematic analysis of all the capital strict works of European composers in their historical sequence.'

This autobiography was written at a time when Moussorgsky was ill, struggling in vain to finish his operas 'Khovanshchina' and the 'Sorochintsi Fair,' and when he was seeing the lone work of his which had won him a measure of fame, 'Boris Godounov,' ruthlessly mutilated in performance and gradually dropping out of the repertory. It was intended for publication abroad; and in it he tried to show himself and his compositions in the best possible light. In short, the autobiography is a pathetic rather than a trustworthy document, which, until lately, Moussorgsky's biographers mistakenly accepted at its face value. The story of what the boy learnt from Father Kroupsky, for instance, was declared grossly exaggerated by Kroupsky himself. And so the story of Moussorgsky's childhood may be substantially true, but it may also be very much embellished. We have no means of checking it.

Boyhood and Youth

The sequence of events, however, is accurately given. After a happy childhood, in his native village, Modeste, at the age of ten, was taken with his brother Philaret to Petersburg, and after two years at a preparatory school the two boys entered the school of the cadets of the Guards.

We have a description of conditions at that school from the pen of a singer, Kompaneisky by name, who was there three or four years after Moussorgsky (whose friend he became later) had left. And it makes one shudder to think of young Moussorgsky, a boy of thirteen who had spent most of his life in the country, suddenly transferred there. He says that the General commanding the school was very proud of his pupils when they came home drunk on champagne. He did not like to see them rolling through the streets, but when they were brought home in a carriage and pair, overcome by champagne, he thought well of them. When he saw Moussorgsky reading or studying, he used to say: 'My dear boy, what kind of an officer will you make?' The cadets were concerned only with gambling or drinking or having expedient affairs with ladies of the nobility or wives of rich merchants. And so Moussorgsky acquired less a taste than a craving for alcohol, which later was to break out despite the efforts he made to resist it.

His skill as a pianist and also as a singer, as well as his charm and his genial disposition, made him popular with his comrades; and when in 1856 he joined the Preobrajensky Regiment, he continued in great request. Borodin, who first met him at that time, has left us a remarkable pen-portrait of him:

'He was a true little fop, all spick and span in a well-fitting uniform, well groomed, his hair carefully brushed, his hands perfectly manicured. He spoke mincingly, inter-larding his sentences with French words. He was very popular with the ladies. At parties, he would sit at the piano, and with coquettish gestures play bits from "Trovatore" or "Traviata," while around him all sat entranced, murmuring "Charmant! Délicieux!"'

Such was, at the age of seventeen, the man who, twelve years later, was to write the grim, deeply stirring opera 'Boris Godounov,' whose uncompromising starkness and daring originality came as a rude shock to polite society and also to the musical world at large.

The 'Kouchka'

That same year, a friend introduced Moussorgsky to Mily Balakirev, his senior by a couple of years, who in 1855 had come to Petersburg from Nijny Novgorod, his native town —a born musician, enthusiastic, gifted, entirely self-taught, eager to follow the lead of Glinka, whose operas 'A Life for the Tsar' and 'Russlan and Lioudmila' (the first examples of national Russian music) he had studied, side by side with Beethoven's symphonies and all the great classical scores he could lay his hands upon; eager, too, to serve the cause of musical art by teaching others and by propagating the music he loved. He had already made a brilliant début, both as a pianist and as a composer, with a fantasy for piano and orchestra. And he naturally became the leader of all the young men who wished to study composition at a time when there were in Russia no professional schools and no competent professional teachers. He had already started giving advice to Cesar Cui (born 1835), who, mainly on the strength of his activities as a journalist and pamphleteer, later gained the reputation of being the leader, jointly with him, of the budding national school. But Moussorgsky was his first actual pupil. A little later, Borodin, Rimsky-Korsakov, and a few less known composers were to form the group, usually called the 'Kouchka' (the mighty handful), of which the leader, after Balakirev, was not Cui really, but the critic Vladimir Stassov.

Many legends obtain of the 'mighty handful,' or 'the Five,' as they are sometimes called, their common ideals, their unfailing understanding of and faith in one another. The truth is that none of them, except Stassov, understood Moussorgsky. And even he began by considering him 'dull, and little short of an idiot'—a view with which Balakirev concurred, although he was fond of his pupil and strove hard to train and direct him. The correspondence between the two testifies to their fondness for one another; and Moussorgsky always remained grateful to Balakirev for his tuition and affection.

Adolescence

In 1858 the call of music became so strong that he resigned his commission in order to devote himself entirely to composition. Soon afterwards, he suffered from what he described as 'a terrible disease'—mental, it would seem, rather than physical; from the description he gives, it must have been mainly a puberty crisis. He soon recovered. The following year he went on a journey to Moscow, where he received his first impressions of the old Russia he was to evoke in his dramatic masterpieces and began, for the first time, to feel 'that he was thoroughly Russian, Russian to the core.'

Before visiting Moscow, he spent some time at Glebovo, the country estate of a wealthy couple—the husband said to have been one of the wealthiest landowners in Russia, the wife an amateur singer who enjoyed a certain reputation. Moussorgsky, apparently, was infatuated with her. This was one of the very few love affairs in his life. He is said to have been in love, in his 'teens, with a cousin of his, but no particulars of this early experience are known. Later, he was to bear a deep, lasting, reverent feeling for Nadejda Opochinina, to whom he inscribed several songs and whose death (in 1874) he commemorated in his beautiful 'Epitaph.' Stassov has vaguely hinted at an affair with a young opera singer, Latysheva by name; and he asserted that these were the only three women for whom Moussorgsky had ever shown 'anything like an amorous feeling.' He always professed to hold the marriage tie in profound horror; and once he said to Lioudmila Shestakova, Glinka's sister: 'If you ever read in the newspaper that I have blown my brains out, you will guess that I was to have been married on the morrow.' His letters to Balakirev testify to his distaste for sex topics; love-songs are few in his musical output; and the 'love interest' in his operas is neither very prominent nor very convincing. In the first version of his masterpiece, 'Boris Godounov,' there was no such interest at all; he introduced a semblance of it in the second version simply because the management of the Imperial Theatre refused to produce an opera in which there was neither a prima donna nor a first tenor.

Early Works and the Civil Service

During the years that followed, Moussorgsky continued to work under Balakirev's guidance, but without any particular purpose. In 1862 he was to confess that 'he felt very far from having found himself.'

The works of this early period—a few songs and piano pieces, sketches for a musical setting of *Œdipus Rex* of which, eventually, very little was composed, and a scherzo for orchestra, successfully performed in January, 1860, at a concert of the Russian Music Society, Anton Rubinstein conducting— show no indication whatever of the line he was to take later.

In 1861 occurred an event that was to alter his prospects considerably. His father had died in 1855, leaving the family, so far as could be foreseen, well provided for. Moussorgsky lived with his mother until 1862, and afterwards, when she had decided, owing to the change in their circumstances brought about by the Imperial Ukase of 19th February, 1861, liberating the serfs (which spelt great difficulties for landowners), to retire to their country estate, with his brother Philaret, by that time married.

Philaret, the administrator of the estate, did not prove equal to his task. Modeste, who had no head for business, vainly tried to help him. In the end very little of the estate remained. Modeste was generously to leave that little to his brother, saying 'he is married and needs the money. I am capable of earning my own living.' Financial difficulties were to compel him in December, 1863, to take up a job as a government clerk. He remained in the service until April, 1867, when he was dismissed. At the end of 1868 he was given a post in another department, lost this a few years later, was reinstated—in a third department—and did not finally leave the service until the end of 1879, fifteen months before his death, drawing a meagre salary and probably working conscientiously at times, but not regularly enough for his chiefs to be able to rely upon him, or even to connive at the liberties he took with his duties.

Mental Development

It has already been mentioned that up to the age of twenty-four he gave absolutely no sign of the individuality he was to assert so strongly a few years later. What led to his finding himself is far from clear. The beginning of the change is to be traced back to the year 1863 when, having, as he says in another autobiographical document, 'set his brains in order and acquired much useful knowledge,' he started life as one of a small community of young men, all of them living together in a flat and intent upon new ideas and new ideals. The names of these young men do not matter: nothing of importance is known of them, and none of them ever achieved anything in life. But what is of interest is the clue Moussorgsky gives us in his autobiography when he speaks of writers and scientists who contributed to the maturing of his mind. No composer, classical or contemporary, really exercised a decisive influence on his outlook and style, although he certainly did owe something to Berlioz, to Glinka, and to Dargomyjsky, the first exponent of realism in Russian opera. Later he was to complain to Stassov that 'whereas he often heard painters or writers express live ideas, musicians, to his knowledge, never did anything of the kind.' The history of Russian thought at that period is that of a steady growth of interest in the people, in their life and fate; and also in true-to-life, or realistic, methods in art. All the people whom Moussorgsky mentions in his autobiography and letters—Grigorovich, Turgeniev, Pissemsky, the novelists; Lamansky and Kostomarov, the historians; and Kavelin, the sociologist and psychologist, among others—may have done far more to help Moussorgsky to find himself than any composer could have done. This, of course, does not mean that they directly influenced the formation of his musical style, but they certainly influenced his outlook. He was led to enquire more and more into the properties of the elements of music—of rhythms and harmonies and melodic patterns—and to go straight for the means of expression that he found most suitable, however unusual they happened to be.

Songs and a Tone Poem

One of his first notions, after joining the community, was to compose an opera on the subject of 'Salammbo' (a Russian translation of Flaubert's famous novel had just appeared). He worked at it at irregular intervals until 1866, then abandoned it. The reason he gave, years later, to Kompaneisky for this decision was: 'It would have been useless anyhow: we have had enough of the East with Servo's "Judith." Art is no mere play, and time is precious.' This meant, Kompaneisky rightly points out, that he did not believe himself, or any Russian, capable of penetrating beneath the surface of Eastern music; and so he steered clear of it, deriving the elements of his style almost exclusively from the folk music of Russia. Nevertheless, the music he wrote for 'Salammbo' comprised much that was racy enough, and rich enough in dramatic significance, to be used again in the final version of 'Boris Godounov.'

In 1864 he composed the first of those admirable songs in which he evokes, most movingly and convincingly, the character and fate of the Russian peasants, and which to this day remain without parallel in the musical repertory: 'Kallistrat,' a picture of a ragged, philosophical peasant boy; and also a lyrical song, 'Night,' whose harmonic texture is as attractive as it is original. The wonderful 'Peasant's Lullaby' followed in 1865. He had found his path at last. But that same year his mother died. The loss affected him terribly. That he sought solace in drink is hardly to be doubted, for in the autumn he collapsed under an attack of *delirium tremens*. He was persuaded to leave the 'commune' and again to take up his quarters at his brother's home, where he lived until the autumn of 1868.

He made a speedy recovery. The following two years were marked by the composition of a few fine songs ('Savishna' and 'Hopak' among others): of a choral 'The Rout of 'Sennacherib,' which was performed at Petersburg in March, 1867, Balakirev conducting; and of a first draft of a tone-poem which eventually became the 'Night on the Bare Mountain' as now known—the only orchestral work of any magnitude that he ever turned out.

'I inscribed it to Balakirev, by request,' he wrote in July to Rimsky-Korsakov. 'I am very pleased with it, and the innovations in it should please all thoughtful musicians, although it contains things which will make Cui advise me to attend a harmony class, and other things which would lead to my being expelled from that class.' Balakirev, apparently, found much to criticise in the score. In September, Moussorgsky wrote to him:

'I was hurt by your attitude to my work—which I regard as perfectly satisfactory. It is the first big one with which I come forth. Now this feeling has vanished. But whether you agree to have it performed or not, I refuse to alter the form or the treatment, which correspond exactly to my views and feelings.'

The work was not performed then, or even during Moussorgsky's lifetime. It was published, after his death, in a drastic revision by Rimsky-Korsakov; and the genuine text was not made available until quite lately. Moussorgsky attempted to make use of it in two ill-fated works: the opera 'Mlada,' for which he was commissioned in 1872 by Gedeonov, the manager of the Imperial Opera, to compose one act, the other acts being entrusted to Borodin, Rimsky-Korsakov, and Cesar Cui—a foolish scheme that fell through after the four composers had wasted a good deal of time over it—and the comic opera 'The Sorochintsi Fair,' begun in 1874 but not carried very far.

The Approach to 'Boris'

The year 1868 was, in many respects, one of the most eventful in his life. He wrote some of his most characteristic songs, including the first of the delightful 'Nursery,' that matchless set of evocations of childhood. He set to music one act of Gogol's comedy 'The Marriage'—an undertaking that marks a new phase in his progress towards the directness and pregnancy of expression in dramatic music which had become his ideal. He began his masterpiece, 'Boris Godounov.' And, financial difficulties having compelled his brother to give up his Petersburg house, he went to live with his friends, Alexander Opochinin and Nadejda, Alexander's sister, for whom his reverent, tender feelings have already been mentioned. He was to spend three happy years in this new home.

It was on 11th June, 1868, that he began work on 'The Marriage,' very much under the stimulus he had received Dargomyjsky's opera 'The Stone Guest,' then in process of composition, and greatly admired by Balakirev's circle, most of whose members, until then, had shown scant respect for Dargomyjsky's music and personality. The 'Stone Guest' aimed at a simplicity and realism in expression which fired their enthusiasm. Moussorgsky's object, in 'The Marriage,' was to capture in his setting 'those changes of intonation which are for ever cropping up in human speech.' He said in a letter to Rimsky-Korsakov:

'If you forget all operatic conventions and admit the principle of musical discourse carried out in all simplicity, then "The Marriage" is an opera. If I have managed to render the straightforward expression of thoughts and feelings, as it takes place in ordinary speech, and if my rendering is artistic and musicianly, then the deed is done.'

He finished this first act, in vocal score form, within twenty-seven days. He was delighted with it. Not so the other members of the circle, who, after this first act had been performed in private in Cui's home, regarded it as a daring experiment and a paradoxical curio rather than as a success from the 'artistic and musical' point of view—Stassov alone dissenting.

Moussorgsky toyed a while with the notion of continuing with 'The Marriage,' then gave it up. He feared, he explained to Rimsky-Korsakov, the danger of 'lapsing into uniformity of inflexion.' To Glinka's sister, Lioudmila Shestakova (who by that time had become, and was to remain, one of his best loved friends) he had written, shortly after the completion of the first act:

'If God grants me health and strength, I shall have a lot to say—but after "The Marriage" is finished. I have now crossed the Rubicon. "The Marriage" is a cage in which I must remain imprisoned until I have learnt my lesson. What I want to do is to make my characters speak on the stage as they would in real life, and yet write music which will be thoroughly artistic.'

But the strongest reason for his deciding to give up this work was that in the autumn his friend, Professor Nikolsky, gave him the idea of turning Pushkin's tragedy, 'Boris Godounov,' into an opera—an idea which set his imagination aflame and drove everything else out of his mind.

'Boris Godounov' and 'Khovanshchina'

He started work in the autumn, adjusting Pushkin's play to suit his own requirements, and carrying on at such a pace that by December, 1869, the opera was ready. He submitted it to the management of the Imperial Opera a few months later, and forthwith started casting around for subjects for other operas. He thought of Pushkin's 'The Captain's Daughter.' Stassov submitted the plan of another libretto, which interested him a while, but was soon cast aside. He wrote three more numbers of 'The Nursery,' and the satirical songs 'The Peep-Show' and 'The Seminarist.' In February, 1871, the news came that the committee of the Imperial Opera had rejected 'Boris Godounov.' They could make neither head nor tail of that opera in which there were no

E

first tenor, no prima donna, no arias or ensembles, no ballets, no 'numbers' of any kind for the soloists—practically nothing but recitative, dialogues, and choral ensembles; and written, moreover, in a musical style thoroughly unlike anything within their experience. Moussorgsky had no option but to remodel his work, in the hope that a revised version would satisfy them. So he added a whole act in which prima donna and the first tenor could fulfil expectations and the desired love-duet take place. He introduced more 'singing,' in the usual sense of the word, in most of the other scenes and cut out certain episodes which might have displeased the State censorship. In short, he did his best to meet the management's views without betraying his own ideals. The revision took up most of his time during 1871 and 1872. In the autumn of 1871, his stay with the Opochinins came to an end, and he and Rimsky-Korsakov took a room together. They shared the writing-table (Rimsky-Korsakov was engaged in composing 'The Maid of Pskov') and took turns to use the piano—an arrangement rendered practicable by the fact that their respective duties called them away from home part of the time.

In May, 1872, the committee of the Imperial Opera met again to consider the matter of 'Boris Godounov.' In June, Stassov gave Moussorgsky the notion of composing a second national and historical opera, 'Khovanshchina,' which pleased him so that he started planning a libretto forthwith. By the time the committee had finally rejected 'Boris,' he was hard at work on the new scheme. He felt more than ever sure of his purpose and at the height of his creative powers. He wrote to Stassov:

'The quest for artistic beauty for its own sake is sheer puerility—is art in its nonage. The goal of the artist should be to study the most subtle features of human beings and of humanity in the mass. To explore and conquer these unknown regions, and find therein a health-giving pabulum for the minds of all men, that is the duty and the joy of joys.

And that is what in *our* "Khovanshchina" we shall try to achieve.'

'Boris' Performed

And so his enthusiasm for the new plan helped him to react against his cruel disappointment. Meanwhile, his friends and admirers started taking steps to make 'Boris' known. On 5th February, 1873, three scenes from the opera were produced on the stage of the Imperial Opera, at the benefit performance of the stage manager, Kondratiev, with great success.

Plans for further partial performances were made. The publishing rights were acquired by Bessel, who forthwith announced the opening of a subscription to the forthcoming vocal score. Moussorgsky's interest in 'Khovanshchina' kept on growing. But despite these favourable omens, the year was to be a black one for him. During the summer he fell a victim to his craving for alcohol. He sold his belongings, and more than once disappeared on drunken orgies, to the great distress of his friends. How far his extreme grief at the death of the young architect Victor Hartmann, whom he held in deep affection, was responsible for this collapse can only be surmised. He was as loyal in his friendships as he was affectionate and sensitive. Four years later, the death of another close friend, the singer Petrov, was to distress him even more deeply.

The crisis was a short one. In the autumn, great news came. Julia Platonova, who had taken part in the 'Boris' scenes given the year before, was entitled to a benefit performance, had insisted that this should consist of 'Boris,' and the management had been compelled to agree. Soon work began; and 'Boris' was produced on 27th January, 1874. It impressed the audiences favourably, but displeased the critics and the influential members of the public. Of Moussorgsky's comrades, the only one who realised the greatness of his achievement was Stassov. Balakirev had offended him by sharp criticisms proffered in public. Cui wrote a disparaging, and indeed malicious, account of it which wounded him to the quick. Rimsky-Korsakov, as he was to explain later, both 'loved the work for its originality and impressiveness, and hated it for the clumsiness and illiteracy it betokened.' However fond they were of the man—whose personality and disposition were most attractive, to whose sincerity and simplicity and honesty all paid tribute, and who always proved as genuine in his feelings and actions as in his artistic convictions—they could not follow the composer along his chosen path. His innovations were too bold for them, his ignorance of conventions too sweeping. He, in turn, began to suspect their genuineness. From that time on he felt isolated from all the men—except Stassov—who had been closest to him, and never confided in them again. Maybe he had felt this even earlier: from 1872 on, practically all those letters of his which have been preserved are to Stassov or to women friends (his correspondence with Golenist-chev-Koutouzov, the poet, with whom he shared rooms from 1873 to 1875, was recently discovered, but is not yet published).

From Old Friends to New

The performances of 'Boris Godounov' continued at irregular intervals. Much had been cut out at the start, further excisions were made again and again. Twenty-six took place from 1874 to 1881, and after that the work was withdrawn and remained forgotten until after Moussorgsky's death. The financial results were not very satisfactory. He received the usual royalties from the theatre, but from his publisher only instalments on account of the small sum (six hundred paper roubles—less than twenty pounds) for which he had sold the publishing rights. Nor did his other published works ever bring in fees worth mentioning.

He must have had means—very small means—of his own,

judging by one preserved letter of 1876 in which he asks for funds to be remitted to him. But he seems to have been dependent mainly on his meagre salary as a government clerk. He found new friends: first Golenistchev-Koutouzov, the author of the poems of the two splendid sets, 'Songs and Dances of Death' and 'Sunless,' which Moussorgsky composed between 1874 and 1876; and a certain Paul Naoumov, at whose house he went to live in 1875, and who, being addicted to drink, is said to have exercised a bad influence on him.

The evidence now available from a great number and variety of trustworthy sources makes it quite clear that during the following years his fits of intemperance grew worse and more frequent. More than once he struggled gamely to resist and concentrate upon the work that meant so much to him, but in vain: he was foredoomed to reap the bitter harvest of the seed sown during his brief military career.

Whether this affected the quality of his creative imagination is doubtful: in the music he composed during the last few years of his life there is much that is as splendid and pregnant as anything he had composed before. But that it affected his capacity for sustained and orderly work is shown by the erratic way in which he, who had made so fine a job of the libretto of 'Boris' carried on with 'Khovanshchina,' vainly struggling to build up a consistent plot, and wasting much of his time on planning, and often actually composing, scenes which he eventually had to discard.

It is true that the task he had undertaken was tremendous, and that to do justice to his subject as he had conceived it a trilogy rather than one single opera would have been required (as was remarked by the Russian critic, Karatygin).

He was also aiming at carrying his search for 'artistic and musical' equivalents of human speech further. In December, 1876, he wrote to Stassov:

'I foresee a new kind of melody, which will be the melody

of life. With great pains I have achieved a type of melody evolved from that of speech. Some day, all of a sudden, the ineffable song will arise, intelligible to one and all. If I succeed, I shall stand as a conqueror in art—and succeed I must.'

Further to complicate matters, in 1874 he began another opera, on a subject derived from one of Gogol's Ukrainian tales, 'The Sorochintsi Fair.' He worked at this at irregular intervals, gave it up 'because he felt that, being a Great Russian, he could never grasp the innermost subtleties of Ukrainian intonation,' resumed it, and to the end of his life tried in vain to carry both it and 'Khovanshchina' through.

Final Difficulties

For many reasons (not all of them clear to the present day) his friends were unable to do much for him. He was in great demand in certain circles as the composer of an opera that had created a sensation, and also as an accompanist—especially at charity concerts and at parties, where he found many opportunities to indulge in his craving. One of the singers whose accompaniments he played was Daria Leonova, who took the part of the Hostess in 'Boris.' The friendship between them grew steadily. In 1879, shortly after completing a world-tour, she planned one through South Russia and invited him to join her. Stassov, Balakirev, and all their circle were appalled, and vainly tried to dissuade him from 'thus disgracing himself.' They felt sure that he was being made to play an unworthy part. The tour took place. It was, according to his own account, most successful in all respects: in actual fact, it was but a moderate success artistically and financially. However, he came back to Petersburg delighted with his experiences (never before had he been on a long journey, nor seen southern skies) and full of plans for new instrumental works inspired by his impressions—but only a couple of mediocre piano pieces materialised.

At the end of 1879 he was dismissed the service. Leonova engaged him as accompanist and adviser to her singing classes. He accepted, to the distress and indignation of his old friends. It is impossible to tell how far their disapproval was justified. Leonova, while obviously aware of the prestige conferred upon her classes by the collaboration of the composer of 'Boris Godounov,' seems to have genuinely done her best to befriend and help Moussorgsky in his appalling difficulties; and possibly the attitude of his censors was not altogether free from a kind of vicarious snobbery.

However, most of them did their best to help him too. One group started, in January, 1880, making him an allowance of 100 roubles a month to enable him to finish 'Khovanshchina.' A few weeks later, another group provided a monthly allowance of 80 roubles, for him to finish 'The Fair.' Thus he was made to stick to the impossible task of continuing with both operas jointly. He kept hard at work throughout the year 1880, and for a while it seemed that he might win through. But on 12th February, 1881, he suddenly fell ill—with epilepsy, according to his doctor's report. He was taken to hospital, and under treatment his condition improved slightly. He continued to think of his plans for future work, and to show the cheerfulness and optimism which had always been part and parcel of his nature. Then paralysis set in, and he died, painlessly, on 28th March, 1881.

Posthumous Misfortune

Thus ended the tragedy of his life. A merciful dispensation of Providence had enabled him to bear his burden and face his difficulties with simple, unfailing courage, and even, it would seem, to find happiness in the pursuit of his ideals and also in his artistic achievements, whose greatness nobody realised until much later.

He was given an impressive funeral. After he had been laid to rest in the great Alexander Nevsky cemetery, close by Glinka's tomb, Stassov and Rimsky-Korsakov under-took the task of preparing his manuscript works for publication. And the story—unparalleled in the whole course of musical history—of the fortune of his output after his death is so closely bound up with the story of his own fortune, and so very illustrative of the evil fate that had always dogged him, that a few words must be devoted to it.

A number of posthumous works appeared, most of them drastically edited by Rimsky-Korsakov; the editing was imperative for the unfinished, ill-proportioned 'Khovansh-china,' but not so for works such as the 'Songs and Dances of Death,' for instance, which had received their final form at his own hands. Other works, like 'The Marriage,' were not published until much later. In 1896, Rimsky-Korsakov, convinced that it would be possible to amend the 'illiterate' music of 'Boris Godounov' without impairing its beauties, submitted it to a drastic revision, which appeared in 1896; and in this revision the long-neglected work (very much abridged, as before) was produced in 1904. Eventually, it became world-famous. Rimsky-Korsakov's second revision (1908) restored the portions of the 1874 edition left out of the first. Moussorgsky's original sank deeper and deeper into oblivion, despite the impassioned protests of a few people in France who, having studied the 1874 edition, proclaimed that the revision did not give a true picture of Moussorgsky's genius, and that the real 'Boris' was incomparably finer. Very slowly this view gained ground, but only in 1928 was the full score of the genuine 'Boris' issued by the Russian State Publishing Department—the first volume of an edition of all Moussorgsky's works exactly as written by him, under the editorship of Paul Lamm.

Moussorgsky once wrote to Rimsky-Korsakov: 'With whatever shortcomings my music is born, with them it must live if it is to live at all.' It is to be hoped that this right of the artist to be judged by his own utterances will be acknow-ledged by all. Now that his output is available at last in its genuine form, there is no excuse for singing his songs or performing his 'Boris' except as written by him, thereby putting an end to a state of things which one would have thought would long since have given rise to protests throughout the world of art. It is high time for Moussorgsky's genius—now acknowledged by all—to come into its own.

BIBLIOGRAPHY

Of late, so much new information on Moussorgsky's life has cropped up in Russia, and the older information has turned out to be so scanty and inaccurate, that not one of the books on him, big or small, published in other countries is of the slightest use to students of his biography, and only the most recent Russian books are reliable. The following are of outstanding value:

MOUSSORGSKY, M. P.: *Letters and Documents*. With a preface and notes by ANDREI RIMSKY-KORSAKOV. (Moscow, State editions, 1932.)

MOUSSORGSKY, M. P.: *Articles and Materials*. Edited by Y. KELDYSH and V. YAKOVLEV. (Moscow, State editions, 1932.)

Boris Godounov, by various authors. (Moscow, State editions, 1930.)

Of the many editions of *Boris Godounov* now on the market the only one giving the full genuine text in strict accordance with the autograph manuscripts is the Lamm edition (Russian State editions—Oxford University Press.) The Lamm edition of the songs—unfortunately not provided with English translations—is the only one giving all the songs in their genuine form.

GIOACCHINO ANTONIO ROSSINI

BORN 29 February 1792   DIED 13 November 1868

By Francis Toye

Boyhood and Youth

Rossini, the son of the municipal trumpeter of Pesaro (an officer that corresponds approximately to our own town crier), showed signs of musical genius in very early years. At the age of fourteen he played with something more than competence on the viola and the horn, while his efficiency on the *cembalo* was such that he was often employed at various local theatres to accompany the recitatives and to train the chorus. He was even better known, perhaps, as a boy-singer, and, more important still (though in all probability few people realised the fact), he had written a considerable amount of music: a song for soprano and some duets for horn intended for him and his father, who, in addition to municipal trumpeting, played that instrument in the local theatre. He had even composed a collection of isolated operatic numbers which were good enough, with some slight revision, to be successfully produced half a dozen years later in Rome as the opera 'Demetrio e Poblio.'

All this would have been remarkable enough in any boy of fourteen, but it was doubly so in young Rossini, whose musical instruction up to that time had been of the most rudimentary description. His aptitude for singing he probably owed in the first instance to his mother, originally a seamstress, who knew little about music but who seems to have been a natural singer of talent. He did not get any kind of serious teaching on the *cembalo* or in composition until he was twelve years old, as the masters provided for him before that date were, to put it mildly, unsatisfactory. Probably the most significant musical influence in his boyhood was exercised by a priest, Don Malerbi, who, in addition to coaching him in singing, first instilled into young Gioacchino that enthusiasm for Mozart and Haydn which was to remain with him throughout his life.

Moreover, the circumstances of his boyhood were scarcely conducive to study of any kind. His father, commonly known as 'Vivezza,' owing to his gay and impulsive disposition, was a fiery republican continually getting into trouble with the authorities for his advanced opinions. This eventually led to the loss of his modest municipal appointment, and he and his wife earned a precarious living by seeking employment in various small theatres in and around Bologna. In their absence Gioacchino was left at Pesaro in the charge of his aunt and grandmother. Nominally he was supposed to be receiving some kind of education in reading, writing and arithmetic, and even in the elements of music, but in practice he seems to have done little except get himself into mischief. An uncommonly high-spirited boy, his vitality manifested itself in a naughtiness probably unique in the annals of great masters of music. Various methods were tried to curb it, including apprenticeship to a blacksmith, but till his tenth or eleventh year nothing had any effect.

By the time, however, that his parents settled definitely in Bologna (1804) he was more or less a reformed character, and two years later, when his voice broke, he studied not only the 'cello but also counterpoint at the Liceo Musicale with something very like diligence. His teacher, Mattei, a pupil of the illustrious Padre Martini, was a pedant who believed fanatically in the virtues of strict counterpoint, and Gioacchino always said he had learnt more from the scores of Haydn and Mozart than from all Mattei's teaching.

In return Mattei nicknamed him 'Il Tedeschino,' or the Little German. Nevertheless the authorities were sufficiently satisfied with his academic progress to entrust him with the writing of a cantata on the occasion of the annual prize-giving in 1808, when he himself received a medal for counterpoint. Moreover, before or about this time he wrote much music of value : five agreeable string quartets, some orchestral variations and two overtures of which the second was subsequently attached to his first opera.

He finally left the Liceo in 1810, not, as is usually said, because Mattei told him that he now knew enough to write operas, if not church music, but because it became increasingly necessary for him to provide for his father and mother. Besides, in the autumn he received a letter from Venice asking whether he would go there and write a one-act opera. His answer was to go at once; it was his first real chance.

The First Operas

Fortunately for Rossini his first opera, 'La Cambiale di Matrimonio,' was a success, though the singers thought that he attached too much importance to the orchestra. It led to his being commissioned to write several one-act operas of the same kind, of which one, 'Il Signor Bruschino,' has acquired fame as exemplifying Rossini's love of a practical joke. Thinking, it is said, that the manager had purposely palmed off on him a bad libretto owing to his youth and inexperience, he is reported deliberately to have played every kind of trick with the score, writing impossible passages for the singers, and so on. In fact the story is not true, as anyone who reads the score of the charming little opera will immediately see for himself.

Almost immediately afterwards, Rossini produced the work destined to establish him as a composer of real importance. This was 'Tancredi,' a serious full-dress opera this time, based on Voltaire's romantic tragedy. *Opera seria*, as the Italians called it, was a highly conventionalised form, and 'Tancredi,' though we should probably find it stilted nowadays, was welcomed as exceptionally fresh and original. It contains in fact almost the only tender love music that Rossini ever wrote, and the Venetians adored it. One of the tunes, the famous 'Di tanti palpiti,' became so popular that the whole of Venice is said to have sung snatches of it from morning till night. Once in the Law Courts the public had to be ordered to stop humming it.

In the same year, 1813, only two and a half months later, Rossini was fortunate enough to win a success, if possible even more pronounced. This time it was a comic opera, 'L'Italiana in Algèri,' which positively took Venice by storm. Never, people said, had there been such sparkling, exciting music. Their enthusiasm was not unjustified, for, despite a rather silly libretto, 'L'Italiana' still seems as fresh as ever. True, there is no trace of sentiment in it, but the high spirits and sense of fun are irresistible.

The success of two such strongly contrasted operas as 'Tancredi' and 'L'Italiana' gave Rossini undisputed musical primacy in that part of Italy. The public, accustomed to the facility indispensable to an Italian opera composer at the time, may not have been so astonished as we are at the production of two such diverse masterpieces in less than six months. But the originality of them must have appeared even more clear. Besides, Rossini was at least as popular a person as he was composer. He was twenty-one; he was good-looking and witty. All the ladies fell in love with him, and his various love affairs were discussed almost as much as his operas. By common consent he had become the most famous and popular figure in Venice.

'The Barber of Seville'

Three years had sufficed to turn Rossini from a promising student into one of the most famous of contemporary Italian composers. Milan now wanted him, and he produced two operas there, neither of which was conspicuously successful. Nor was the *opera seria* with which he again tempted fortune in Venice at the end of 1814. The escape of Napoleon from Elba immediately threw Italy into a ferment, reviving the old political troubles with which he had been only too familiar in his childhood, and cannot have helped matters. It must have been with a sense of relief that he accepted a contract in the spring of 1815 to go to Naples.

Here, too, all was not plain sailing by any means. The Neapolitans considered Rossini a foreigner, and they despised foreigners because they thought that only Neapolitans had any real knowledge of music. Further, the impresario of the opera, one Barbaia, was renowned for his ruthless and autocratic methods, and especial regard had to be paid to the idiosyncrasies and whims of Isabella Colbran, who was his prima donna and also his mistress. Rossini was fortunate enough to win the confidence of this powerful couple almost at once, so that when, towards the end of the year, he produced his first opera for Colbran he was able to have his own way in two very important matters of detail. Hitherto the recitatives in opera had been accompanied on the *cembalo*. In this opera, 'Elisabetta,' Rossini provided an orchestral accompaniment. More important still, he wrote down for the first time *all* the notes to be sung by the singers. Experience had taught him that the improvisations in which the singers of the time used to indulge might be good or might be bad, but that in either event they were liable to alter the character of the music. So, taking advantage of Barbaia's prestige and Colbran's popularity, he launched as an innovation what has since become an accepted practice.

One of the terms of Rossini's contract was that he should be allowed on certain occasions to leave Naples. He took advantage of this in November to go to Rome, where he wrote for the Argentina Theatre the work by which he is mainly remembered to-day : the immortal 'Barber of Seville.'

He had not gone to Rome with this particular opera in view; the choice of Beaumarchais's play as a subject was almost the result of an accident. It is impossible here to tell the whole interesting story of the birth of this astonishing masterpiece, or to give more than the barest outlines of its chequered infancy. Those who are interested will find a full description in the fourth chapter of my book on Rossini.

Apparently Rossini wrote the music in less than a fortnight. True, he made use of a few ideas from previous operas and appropriated bodily the 'storm music' from another. People sometimes imagine that he did not write a new overture because the overture now associated with 'The Barber of Seville' had already done service on two other occasions. This, however, is not the case. 'The Barber' originally had an overture of its own which has since been lost. In short, the time occupied in the composition of this opera is one of the standard miracles of music; it hardly seems possible that the notes could be written down in two weeks, much less thought of. The feat becomes all the more remarkable in view of the quality of the music. 'The Barber' has remained for more than a hundred years one of the most popular comic operas in the world, perhaps the most popular. The musicians, headed by Beethoven and Wagner, have admired it no less than the general public. Not only is the music, with its sparkle, its bustle, its satirical humour, delightful in itself, but it provides just the right interpretation of Beaumarchais's play, with the mocking personality of Figaro dominating the whole.

Yet on its first production on February 20th, 1816, 'The Barber' was practically hissed off the stage by an audience that seems to have gone to the theatre determined to ruin it. The management was excessively unpopular to begin with; the partisans of Paisiello (who had successfully set the same subject to music) were set on finding fault; there was a series of those untoward accidents too often associated with first nights. Rossini was so discouraged that he slipped out of the theatre and went home, where the prima donna, Giorgi Righetti, going round to offer consolation later in the evening, found him apparently asleep. It was almost certainly a pretence, for Rossini was the most nervous and sensitive of men and always did his best to hide his real feelings. But he soon had his revenge. The second performance of 'The Barber' was as successful as the first had been disastrous. From that day it has never looked back.

Work in Italy

During the next five and a half years Rossini's life is little but a chronicle of various operas, the majority of which need not even be specified. His headquarters remained at Naples, where he contrived, as usual, to enjoy himself, consuming large quantities of macaroni and oysters, drinking the agreeable wines of the country, and embarking upon a serious love affair with Isabella Colbran. But he was not idle; far from it. For during the period in question he wrote no less than sixteen operas, mainly for Naples but also for Rome, Milan and other cities.

The first of these that need be mentioned was 'Otello,' a setting of Shakespeare's play, or rather of a travesty of Shakespeare's play, which in its day was regarded as one of the great operas of the world. And indeed there is some beautiful music in it, notably in the last act, but we are never likely to hear it again. A year later (1817) came 'La Cenerentola,' produced in Rome with, in the first instance, results as unfortunate as those of 'The Barber.' This very mundane version of the story of Cinderella is not dead by any means, as those who have heard recent performances in London, Paris or Florence will know for themselves. It is a delicious score, one of the most workmanlike ever penned by the composer, full of fresh musical ideas and of particularly felicitous ensembles.

'Mosè' (1818) and 'Maometto II' (1820), need not detain us, the less because they only exist now in the revised versions subsequently made by the composer for Paris. But 'Mosè' was in its day one of Rossini's most popular works and the famous 'Prayer,' so familiar to our great-grand-parents, took Europe, and even England, by storm; while several of the impressionable young ladies of Naples are said to have been so moved by it that they were afflicted with nervous prostration! Between the two came 'La Donna del Lago' (1819), which is none other than our old friend 'The Lady of the Lake,' an opera that is of interest as foreshadowing certain characteristics of 'William Tell.' But perhaps the most important of all these operas in a sense was 'La Gazza Ladra' or 'The Thieving Magpie,' which Rossini went to Milan to produce in 1817. 'La Gazza Ladra' is not quite a comic opera and not quite an *opera seria*. It may be considered the first ancestor of the school of Realistic Opera which subsequently found so much favour in Italy. There is some splendid music in it, especially the overture, which begins with the then unheard-of innovation of a drum roll. Indeed, most of Rossini's overtures possess an excellence which their gradual reintroduction at our orchestral concerts is again beginning to make evident to modern ears.

In 1822 Rossini's Neapolitan career came to an end with the opera 'Zelmira.' Barbaia, who had gone to Vienna to restore the fortunes of the Kärnthnerthor Theatre, wished Rossini to join him there with his latest opera. What might have been the complication of Rossini's marriage to Isabella Colbran during this very year does not seem to have been a complication at all. On the contrary, everything worked out most satisfactorily, and towards the end of March, Rossini, accompanied by his wife and several members of the Neapolitan company, left Italy for Vienna. It was the first time he had visited a foreign country.

At Home and Abroad

Rossini's music had already acquired a European reputation, but Viennese musical circles were sharply divided as to its

merits. If a good many of the German musicians, headed by
Weber, were hostile, society and the public were almost
unanimous in their enthusiasm, which was in fact often
pushed to extreme lengths. This exaggeration may well
have explained Weber's hostility, for which, as a matter of
fact, he subsequently apologised to Rossini. But Schubert
always liked his music and was far more influenced by it than
is usually realised. Beethoven himself, though he cared little
for the *opere serie*, recognised Rossini's genius as a composer
of comic operas. 'Give us plenty of "Barbers,"' he said
when Rossini, filled with admiration for the 'Eroica' Symphony, went to see him and pay his respects. The meeting
must assuredly be reckoned one of the most dramatic in the
history of music. On the one hand the prematurely aged,
deaf Beethoven living in lonely squalor; on the other Rossini,
young, urbane, witty, the favourite of everybody in Vienna.
Rossini himself was so moved by it that he tried to inaugurate
a subscription to provide Beethoven with more comfortable
quarters, but the Viennese, who had very definite opinions
about Beethoven, refused to support him, and the project
fell through.

Rossini's four months in Vienna were a succession of
festivities and triumphs, so that he was probably glad enough
to pass the summer quietly at his wife's villa just outside
Bologna. He did not produce any new work of importance
till the following year, when the famous opera 'Semiramide'
was performed in Venice at the beginning of February, 1823.
The defects in 'Semiramide,' which are numerous, seem more
obvious to us nowadays than its merits, but at the time it was
considered the greatest opera of the day and has been described
as being to Rossini very much what Austerlitz was to Napoleon. For in this very year no less than twenty-three of his
operas were being performed in different countries—and he
was only thirty-two!

At that time England stood in much the same relationship
to the world of music as the United States do now. It was

the country where musicians went primarily to make money. So it is hardly surprising that such a popular figure as Rossini had now become should have been invited to London, where he arrived early in December. The ostensible object of his visit was to write an opera for the King's Theatre, but for one reason or another the opera never materialised. He was wholly successful, however, about money, for by singing at parties, accompanying Isabella at the piano and so on, he made some 175,000 francs, an enormous sum for those days. London Society welcomed him with open arms during his few months' stay, and he enjoyed the privilege of singing duets with George IV.

Paris and 'William Tell'

On his way to London, Rossini had stopped in Paris, where he now returned in August, 1824. Paris was at that time the centre of European culture and, though on personal, nationalistic, and even musical grounds some French musicians were hostile to Rossini, the Court and the Government were extremely desirous to have the most brilliant composer of the day in residence there. They established him in general command of the Théâtre Italien, devoted, as its name indicates, to the production of Italian operas, and later, when this contract came to an end, they invented for him the extraordinary post of Composer to His Majesty and Inspector General of Singing at a yearly salary of 20,000 francs.

Except for an insignificant trifle, Rossini never wrote, probably never intended to write, an Italian opera for Paris. His goal was the Opéra itself, where performances had to be in French. With this in view he took considerable trouble to study not only the French language but the idiosyncrasies of French taste and French singing. The first results of this were apparent in 'Le Siège de Corinthe' (1826) and 'Moïse' (1827), revised and considerably elaborated versions of 'Maometto II' and 'Mosè' respectively. 'Moïse' in particular has some splendid music, notably in the choruses, but the principal interest of these operas to us is historical, in that they were the forerunners of the school of Grand Opera subsequently identified with the Opéra in general and Meyerbeer in particular. Then, in 1828, he produced 'Le Comte Ory,' a work of lighter calibre, which contains some of the most elegant and delightful music that he ever wrote. This too is of great historical importance, in that it influenced and helped to form the characteristics of the whole school of French Comic Opera.

But the climax of Rossini's Paris career, perhaps of his whole career, was the opera 'William Tell' (1829). 'William Tell,' which is, of course, based on Schiller's play of the same name, is unique among Rossini's operas for the conscious trouble he took in writing it. For originality, for carefulness of workmanship, for elaboration of scoring, it stands in a class apart. Verdi, Wagner, and Meyerbeer were all influenced by it. Even to-day the overture, which is in reality a symphonic poem in miniature, remains an acknowledged masterpiece.

Yet 'William Tell' never enjoyed the popular success deserved by the qualities of the music. Partly the poor quality of the libretto was to blame; partly the excessive length. On the other hand, to call it a failure, as is sometimes done, is absurd. Headed by Berlioz, the musicians of the world lavished their praises upon it; it secured for the composer the Legion of Honour and a Serenade from the distinguished conductor, Habeneck, and the Conservatoire Orchestra; it achieved five hundred performances in Paris alone during the composer's lifetime.

Still, there can be little doubt that Rossini, accustomed to the applause of the multitude, was disappointed at the result. The Opéra Directorate subsequently turned their main attention to Meyerbeer and contented themselves with giving 'William Tell' in a mutilated form, sometimes indeed only one act. It was on such an occasion as this that the Director, chancing to meet Rossini in the street and thinking to please him, said that the Second Act was being given on that very night. To which Rossini, who was as caustic as he was witty, merely replied, 'What! the whole of it?'

The Latter Years

As the whole world knows, Rossini never wrote another opera after 'William Tell'—one of the most extraordinary phenomena in the history of art. He was only thirty-seven years old, at the very apex of his fame. The problem of 'the Great Renunciation,' as it has been called, has provided material for much speculation and I myself have fully discussed it elsewhere. Speaking generally it may be said that it was in part the result of accident, in part of circumstances, and in part of deliberate volition.

When Rossini left Paris for a long rest he had every expectation of writing another opera in accordance with the terms of his contract. But in 1830 there came the Revolution in Paris which overthrew the Government and incidentally destroyed the contract. Gradually, moreover, his health began to give way. The dissipation of his early years coupled with the intense strain of his working life— he had written more than thirty operas in twelve years!— had enfeebled his nerves to an extent that eventually became pathological. For instance, his first journey in a train prostrated him for days, and the news of the death of someone he cared for, of his adored mother especially, affected him like a serious illness. Furthermore, he undoubtedly felt that his day was done, that people were far more interested in music like that of Meyerbeer, which he disliked, while remaining on friendly terms with the composer himself. He was out of sympathy with the revolutionary spirit of the times; he disapproved of the new orientation of the Italian theatre, and above all he bitterly deplored the gradual decline in the standard of singing. Rossini was not exactly lazy but he needed a stimulus to exertion, and the stimulus was lacking. He had made enough money to live on; he had no children. Why bother? Perhaps in reality he acted wisely. Heine thought so and considered his retirement a sign of genius as distinct from mere talent.

He did, in fact, write two other major works, one, the well-known 'Stabat Mater' some ten years later, and the other, the 'Petite Messe Solennelle,' at the very end of his life. Neither of these works is written in a style considered appropriate nowadays to ecclesiastical music, but the 'Stabat Mater,' has some beautiful numbers, and the Mass, though less well known, is in its way a masterpiece. Rossini called it 'the last mortal sin of my old age' and commended it and himself to his Maker in what is assuredly one of the most curious dedications ever penned.

The facts of Rossini's life during the thirty-nine years after 'William Tell' are of little interest. He went to Italy and made journeys to several European countries but he still kept Paris more or less as his headquarters. Perhaps the most important event was his separation from Isabella, who had become tiresome and very extravagant, and his increasing intimacy with a reformed demi-mondaine called Olympe Pélissier, whom he subsequently married a year after Isabella's death in 1845. She proved to be the most devoted and self-sacrificing of wives and without her devotion it is more than probable that Rossini would have ended his days in a madhouse.

By the time he returned to settle down in Bologna in 1836, the condition of his nerves had grown definitely worse. He was still able, however, to enjoy life, and during the winter of 1837, which he spent in Milan, his musical parties were the talk of the city. Later he devoted much time and trouble to the reorganisation of the Liceo Musicale at Bologna; he even wrote a little music, completing in fact the 'Stabat Mater,' of which he had written the first six numbers whilst on a journey to Spain nine years previously.

Gradually, however, his health became worse, and a demonstration against him in 1848 on account of his supposed lukewarmness in the cause of Italian independence came as a climax to his trouble. He fled incontinently to Florence, where, during the next seven years, he lived a life of almost complete retirement, exceedingly miserable, in an acute state of neurasthenia, hardly able to taste or assimilate his food and tortured by sleeplessness. In despair Olympe determined at last to remove him to Paris, trusting that the change of environment and doctors might prove beneficial. Her judgment proved right, for after a year or two's drastic treatment, Rossini, if not completely cured, was able once more to find some pleasure in life. He was once again one of the idols of Paris, the father, real or putative, of all the best witticisms; every celebrity who visited the capital made a point of coming to see him. Among these was Wagner, with whom he had a particularly interesting discussion on the past, the present and the future of music. Despite their extreme divergence of views the two men never ceased subsequently to entertain a genuine respect for one another.

For many years Rossini had written no music of any description, but in 1857 he began writing those amusing trifles from some of which Respighi fashioned the ballet known as 'La Boutique Fantasque.' In the first instance they were mainly designed for the famous Saturday evening parties which he gave at his flat in the Rue de la Chaussée d'Antin. Every singer of repute who visited Paris wished to be asked to sing at these, and the fashionables of the city vied with one another to secure invitations. Rossini's Saturday evenings became, indeed, almost as famous as his operas.

During the summer months he retired to a villa he had built for himself at Passy, where he died after a comparatively short illness on November 13th, 1868, attended to the last by the devoted Olympe. He was buried in the first instance in Père Lachaise, but, nineteen years later, at the request of the Italian Government, his remains were removed to the Church of Santa Croce at Florence, the Westminster Abbey of Italy.

He was worthy of the honour, for, though he had never been anything of a hero either in life or art, he was a great musician, more richly endowed by nature, perhaps, than any except the very greatest. No one has ever known better how to embody in music the joy of living. Even to-day, nearly a hundred years since his retirement from professional life, his exuberant vitality and genial laughter surprise and delight us. Essentially a lover of the good things of this world, he never rose to supreme emotional or spiritual heights, but the world has reason to be grateful for the tonic qualities of his sparkling and often highly sensitive music.

BIBLIOGRAPHY

Curzon, Henri de: *Rossini.* (Paris, 1920.)

Derwent, Lord: *Rossini—and some Forgotten Nightingales.* 15s. (Duckworth, 1924.)

Rodiciotti, Giuseppe: *Gioacchino Rossini.* 3 vols. (Tivoli, 1923.)

Toye, Francis: *Rossini; a Study in Tragi-Comedy.* 10s. 6d. (Heinemann, 1934.)

FRANZ PETER SCHUBERT

BORN 31 January 1797   DIED 19 November 1828

By William Glock

Early Years

Franz Schubert was born in Lichtenthal, a suburb of Vienna.
Both his father and his mother had come to Vienna from
Austrian Silesia. The family records can be traced back to
the sixteenth century. Karl Schubert, Franz's grandfather,
was a farmer and local magistrate at Neudorf near Altstadt
(there were thirty-five Neudorfs thereabouts), and in 1780
had erected, on the height above his house, a statue of
'Christ on the Mount of Olives' which excited great admiration. He had thirteen children, of whom nine died young,
and Franz Theodor, the composer's father, was to repeat
that experience almost exactly with his first marriage. The
people of the district were hard-working, serious and strict,
and from them Vienna recruited many of her best officials,
teachers and intellectuals. Franz Theodor, who came to
Vienna as assistant teacher to his brother, became quickly
distinguished for his industry, moral character, stamina and
piety. Elisabeth Vietz, whom he married in 1783, came from
a mountain town called Zuckmantel, which had experienced
several wars and had been burned to the ground six times during two hundred years. Economic progress was impossible,
and when the father, Franz Johann, impoverished by the
Seven Years' War, took desperate steps that led to his ruin,
the sons and daughters were forced to earn their living abroad
and left, one and all, for Vienna.

Life must have been very hard, even for parents accustomed
to denial and adversity. Franz Theodor applied continually
for a better post than that at the parish school 'zu den heiligen

vierzehn Nothelfern,' but government intrigue, and his
extraordinary success in a school that had previously fallen
into extreme disrepute, postponed the fulfilment of his hopes
for many years. The attendance at the Lichtenthal school
had, from no pupils at all, reached 174, and was later to
increase to 300. At this time schoolmasters at the parish
schools in Vienna received no salary. They could have
free lodging in the school, and were entitled to one florin
school-money per month from each pupil. It is unlikely
that schoolmaster Schubert ever earned more than £35 a
year during Franz's childhood.

Little is known of Franz's early years but that he was of a
cheerful, companionable nature, and quickly afforded proof
of his extraordinary gifts. Of his earliest three teachers in
music—his father; Ignaz, the eldest brother (then about
twenty), and Michael Holzer, the parish organist—only the
first could contain his astonishment. He was determined that
all his sons should follow his own profession. Ignaz, who
taught Franz the pianoforte, tells of his surprise when his
young brother declared, after a few months, that he would no
longer need his instruction. Michael Holzer, a good-natured
man of about thirty-five, a notable drinker and a fairly accomplished musician, said that whenever he wished to teach Franz
anything he found that it was known already. He therefore
looked on, and was filled with pride and astonishment.

Many geniuses have had more stubborn instruction. But
few have lived their youth in such an atmosphere of music
as pervaded Vienna at this time, and still fewer have had the
opportunity to gain such practical experience through continual performances in choir and orchestra as Franz Schubert
was now to have.

The possibility of Franz's becoming a choirboy in the
Chapel Royal must have appealed tremendously to his father,
for it meant also a free education at the Imperial Konvikt,
which was the most important boarding school in Vienna.
When, therefore, a vacancy for one boy soprano was an-

nounced, Franz, now nearing his twelfth year, was entered for the examination. The beautiful quality of his voice and his expressive manner of singing had already won him fame in Lichtenthal; in addition, his cleverness and advanced knowledge of music enabled him to surpass easily all the other candidates, who had been making fun of his 'miller's suit.'

The Konvikt

There were places for eighteen choirboys in the Konvikt, of whom ten belonged to the Chapel Royal and eight to the Court Church. As there was a teaching staff of over twenty, the choristers must have formed only a small percentage of the students. Their existence imposed the cultivation of music as a subject and certainly lent an added impulse to its practice, but the Konvikt did not exist only for choirboys. Other subjects were considered of more importance than music.

Though it is unjust, therefore, to criticise the Konvikt for neglecting the musical education of a young genius, it yet remains a striking fact that Schubert did not begin the study of counterpoint until he was over fifteen. An exercise sheet of this time has been preserved, on which four *canti fermi* are written in a shaking hand, that of Salieri; the counterpoint above, in contrasting boldness, show Franz to have been as yet unskilled in the art. Salieri had been deeply impressed by 'Hagars Klage,' a huge composition for voice and pianoforte by Schubert, who, as a consequence, and on account of his blameless reputation, was allowed to go from school alone to take lessons from the famous Italian.

His music master within the Konvikt was Wenzel Rucziczka, whose energy and enthusiasm the school governors were never tired of praising. From him Franz probably learned a good deal, economy of notes, how to write for the voice and to achieve beauty of sound even where striving for the sharpest characterisation. That Rucziczka was a Moravian was doubtless not without importance as well.

Orchestral practices at the Konvikt had been inaugurated by the Director, Dr. Innocenz Lang, who was keenly interested in music. The orchestra numbered twenty-nine players; there were sixteen strings, eight wood-wind, two horns, two trumpets, and percussion. On beautiful summer evenings, walkers returning from the *Basteien* would listen at the opened windows; there were such crowds that the street was impassable, and a mechanic named Hanacek, who lived opposite, brought out every chair in his house for the ladies to sit upon. Franz at first stood behind the leaders of the second violins. The keenness and certainty of his playing at once attracted attention, and won for him the truest and most sensible of all his friends, Josef von Spaun. Franz presently became leader of the orchestra, and often conducted when Rucziczka was absent.

Every evening after supper two overtures and a symphony were performed. The music ranged from Haydn, Mozart and Beethoven to Krommer and Kozeluch, whose works are now forgotten. Schubert used warmly to defend the rather antiquated style of Kozeluch against that of Krommer, whose cheerful and vigorous compositions had won great popularity. His favourite overtures were those to 'Figaro' and 'The Magic Flute'; of the symphonies the two that made the deepest impression on him were the G minor of Mozart and the D major of Beethoven.

The orchestral practices were a continual source of enjoyment, but other circumstances conspired to make life at the Konvikt rigorous. The teachers were strict, unsympathetic Piarist monks, there was no womanly supervision or care whatever, and the food was scanty. Franz's earliest known letter, addressed at the beginning of his last year at the Konvikt to his brother Ferdinand, affords touching proof of this. 'You know,' he says, 'from experience how sometimes one wants to eat a roll and a few apples, and all the more when after a modest dinner one can only look forward to a wretched supper $8\frac{1}{2}$ hours later.' The Bible is then quoted in support of charity, and Franz's irresistible description of himself as 'your loving, poor, hopeful, once again poor, and to be remembered brother' leaves one convinced that the last months were eased to the extent of a few kreutzers by brother Ferdinand.

The *Gymnasium* reports do not confirm the often repeated view that Franz was without talent or interest in less absorbing pursuits than music. Not until his final year do the reports contain any disagreeable details. But upon being offered the Meerfeld Scholarship (the highest honour a choirboy could win) provided that he remedied a '2' for mathematics during his vacation, Franz resolved to leave the Konvikt. The decision expressed more than a distaste for mathematics. Clearly, it was not only his spare time that had become dedicated to music. Josef von Spaun had been generously providing him with manuscript paper, in the utmost secrecy for fear schoolmaster Schubert should come to hear of it. Franz Theodor did, however, make the discovery, and when Schubert was fourteen forbade him the house.

The Dream

This obstinate, unimaginative course must have affected the young composer deeply. After a year Elisabeth Schubert died, and father and son were reconciled at her death-bed. Many years later, after another quarrel and a final reconciliation, Franz wrote the allegory known as *My Dream*.

'I was one of many brothers and sisters. We had a good father and mother. I felt a deep love for them all. One day my father took us to a feast. My brothers became very merry there. But I was sad. My father thereupon came up to me and ordered me to taste the delicious foods. But I could not, and at that my father in anger banished me from his sight. I turned on my heel and with a heart filled with infinite love for those who scorned it, wandered into a far country. For years I was torn between the greatest sorrow and the greatest love.'

Then followed his mother's death. 'From this time

onwards I stayed at home again. Then one day my father led me once more into his pleasure-garden. He asked me if it pleased me. But the garden was altogether hateful to me and I dared not reply. Then he asked me a second time, excitedly, whether I liked the garden. Trembling I told him "No." At that my father struck me and I fled. For the second time I turned away, and, with a heart filled with infinite love for those who scorned it, wandered again into a far country. Through long, long years I sang my songs. But when I wished to sing of love it turned to sorrow, and when I wanted to sing of sorrow it was transformed for me into love.' . . . After a passage of great beauty and vision, the dream concludes: 'My father I saw too, loving and reconciled. He folded me in his arms and wept. And I still more.'

Of Franz's profound suffering there can be no doubt. His decision to leave home and school-teaching, to win freedom though it meant living in crushing poverty, was not taken lightly. But to this we must return later.

Schubert and Salieri

It is tempting to discover in the subjects of Schubert's first vocal compositions at the Konvikt some reaction to his banishment. But possibly such titles as 'The Parricide' and 'The Corpse Fantasia' represent nothing but boyish tastes. Schubert's model in these tremendous ballads of twelve and seventeen movements was Zumsteeg, and through him he was attracted to Schiller, whose predilection for the horrible had once been noticed by Goethe. Zumsteeg had been a great friend of Schiller, had set tremendous stretches of his poetry enthusiastically to music, and was much admired by Haydn for his 'imagination, and fine sense of form.' Schubert imitated, but not slavishly; he must have gained a great deal from such exercise, and above all from the style and character of the music, which was thoroughly German. Soon his energy and invention began to surpass that of his model. It was Salieri who, as has been related, was so impressed by 'Hagar's Lament,' another ballad of the same year modelled on Zumsteeg, that Schubert was allowed to go alone from the Konvikt to study with him. The Italian thereafter devoted his energies to turning Schubert against such things. That Salieri advised him to set the poems of Metastasio to music rather than those of Goethe and Schiller is of little importance. Salieri also found fault with 'Figaro,' and said that the closing scene of the first act of 'Titus' was dramatically quite wrong; but this did not convince even an average talent like Josef Hüttenbrenner, who was a fellow pupil with Schubert. The natural antipathy of Salieri to German poetry was supported by a colossal ignorance of the language, which he excused by saying that he had lived in Germany only half a century; his criticism of Mozart was founded on jealousy. Yet both Schubert and Beethoven before him were attracted to this man. And that Schubert was proud of being his pupil may be seen, for instance, in the inscription of a work of 1815—'X Variations pour le Forte-piano composés par François Schubert, Écolier de Salieri, premier Maître de la chapelle impériale et royale de Vienne. . . .' Two operas of this year also bear the remark, 'pupil of Salieri.'

Metastasio used to let Salieri, when they were alone, de-claim sometimes whole scenes of operas; Salieri says how useful this was, and Metastasio thought it absolutely necessary for all song writers. Both believed that 'well spoken is half sung.' Schubert undoubtedly learned good Italian diction from Salieri, and a certain skill in *opera buffa*. He developed a style, already noticeable in the second subject of the over-ture to his first opera, 'Des Teufels Lustschloss,' which has an individuality apart from the rest of his music.

But development and characterisation and the ability to recognise when a libretto was undramatic, Salieri could not teach. And Schubert had not the ornamental brilliancy and theatrical dash that enabled Rossini to triumph temporarily with libretti almost as poor as Schubert's own. The story of

Schubert's operatic ventures, of his repeated attempts to improve his fortunes at the worst possible time, is perhaps the most depressing of all. The greatest harm Salieri did was to initiate this history of tragic waste, of fine music buried beneath impossible libretti, and of failures that darkened Schubert's days with bitter disappointment.

Before leaving the Konvikt, at the end of October 1813, Schubert had finished his first symphony, in D. It was dedicated to Innocenz Lang. The second subject of the first movement is very much as Mozart would have rendered the theme in the last movement of the 'Eroica.' Schubert had to wait until his fifth symphony, in B flat, to escape stiffness 'like a delightful child overawed into perfect behaviour not by fear or priggishness but by sheer delight in giving pleasure.' But already the instrumentation is individual, especially in the andante. Earlier in the year, he had composed a cantata for his father's name-day festival, which must have surprised Franz himself, for the inscription at the end is 'For my father's name-day!!!'

He now entered the St. Anna Training College. His momentary submission to his father's design for living may be explained as arising from a wish to avoid the seven years' conscription to which every man between the ages of 16 and 45 was liable. In 1814 he became teacher of the lowest class at his father's elementary school in the Säulengasse. The history of the next three years is simple and astonishing almost above any other in the whole of art.

Wonderful Years

Schubert finished 'Des Teufels Lustschloss' in May, 1814. His first Mass, in F, was performed at the Lichtenthal church in October, and was such a success that his father presented him with a five-octave piano and Salieri boasted of him as his pupil. Unable to afford a copyist, Schubert wrote out all the parts himself, of which the string ones alone filled eighty-six pages. It was now, while waiting for a second and more important performance ten days later at the Imperial Church of St. Augustine, that Schubert composed 'Gretchen am Spinnrade.' Goethe, in discussing knowledge that is innate with the poet, says he could, in 'Faust,' know by antici- pation how to describe the hero's gloomy weariness of life and the emotions of love in the heart of Gretchen; and only this, that the inner world is inborn with the genius, can explain the miracle achieved by a youth of seventeen. The marvellous accompaniment, the perfect modulations and absolute dramatic fitness of every detail of the song have excited the wonder of all musicians. With 'Gretchen,' as has often been said, German song was created.

A month previously, Schubert had composed the first movement of the B flat quartet in the unbelievably short time of four and a half hours. This was the prelude to a year of unparalleled creative activity, during which Schubert com- posed 6 operas, 2 Masses, 2 symphonies, 3 sonatas and 144 songs. To describe such productiveness as the result of in- dustry would be nonsensical. There is no documentary evidence of his other activities during the year 1815. Schu- bert's life had become music. It is with astonishment that we remember his six hours' daily instruction of small children in the rudiments of reading, writing and arithmetic, at a yearly salary of 32s.

There is excellent music in the operas. The overture to 'Der Vierjährige Posten,' still frequently played, is delicious; the lightnings in 'Fernando,' the snakes in 'Die Freunde von Salamanka,' and Olivia's 'creeping alone through the rooms,' are depicted with almost Handelian power and realism. In the last-named opera occurs also the melody that Schubert used nine years later for the variations in the octet.

Splendid as much of this music is, the songs, in which Schubert already frequently reaches perfection, are a far greater achievement. Among his thirty settings of Goethe in 1815 are several—'Heidenröslein,' 'Meeresstille,' 'Wanderers Nachtlied,' 'Rastlose Liebe' and 'Erlkönig'—universally

known and celebrated.   The story of Schubert 'whelming'
the Erlkönig on to paper is a familiar one.   He hurried off to
the Konvikt with two friends, Spaun and Mayrhofer, who had
called on him and found him in a state of tense excitement;
and there Rucziczka played through the song, putting in the
vocal line on the piano, and, when exception was taken to
the minor ninths on the words 'Mein Vater!', defended the
music, saying how inevitably it suited the text, how beautiful
it was (not ugly as they said) and how happily resolved.   The
poem of 'Rastlose Liebe' so excited Schubert that he was for
a time in a kind of ecstasy, until he freed himself from its effect
by expressing it in musical form.   In a single day, that of the
anniversary of 'Gretchen am Spinnrade,' he composed eight
songs.

1815 marked a climax.   Such an unceasing urge to create
had never before been known.   Yet in the following year
Schubert wrote 110 songs (of which 'Der Wanderer' is the
most famous), two symphonies—the fourth and fifth, in C
minor and B flat—a Mass, an opera-fragment, and the three
sonatinas for pianoforte and violin.   The record is still
astonishing.   Not until 1817 does his productiveness approach
common standards.   There are no dramatic works, no symphonies, no church music; only one chamber work, three
overtures, two of them in the Italian style and reflecting the
momentary rage for Rossini, forty-seven songs, and seven
pianoforte sonatas.   The centre of interest and experiment
has changed.   Schubert had recently met one or two very
talented pianists, among them J. von Gahy, who became a fine
interpreter of his music and with whom Franz was especially
fond of playing pianoforte duets.   Some of his friends
possessed the most modern instruments, and Schubert was
inspired by their fresh possibilities; he also won a close
acquaintance with contemporary pianoforte music.   There
was thus every incentive for this first grand essay in a medium
that Schubert was to enrich with so many noble and magnificent works.

The Significance of the Sonatas

That sixty-five pianoforte sonatas were being published every year around 1800, and in 1850 only three, might be said to epitomise musical history in the first half of the nineteenth century. Schubert was the last great composer of pianoforte sonatas.

His unshakable earnestness is nowhere more clearly seen than in his determination to solve the most serious and difficult artistic problems, while his contemporaries in Vienna were busy writing short lyrical pieces with attractive new titles. He felt an overpowering responsibility. His incessant striving to balance matter and form satisfactorily was presided over by the perfect examples of the previous generation. The figure of Beethoven, above all, inspired him, but to an equal extent weighed him down throughout his years of mature creation. Goethe maintained that he 'rid' himself of Shakespeare by writing 'Goetz von Berlichingen' and 'Egmont'; but the only musician whose greatness is comparable with that of Shakespeare was too immanent, both in time and place, for Schubert not to have remained fundamentally affected.

The opinion that Schubert's instrumental music is weak in form has acquired an almost legendary power. It rests partly upon a too rigid conception. His finest movements have continuity and inevitableness; they are not protracted to any greater length than the magnificent themes demand. His music has not the tension of Beethoven's. Contrasts, to Schubert, were not dramatic, but simply existed. He was led therefore to fill his movements with a richness of content, and was dramatic not in conflict, but in the development of a single idea to its highest pitch.

The neglect of Schubert's sonatas, in which may be discovered perhaps the central significance of his genius, though not its most perfect expression, is very revealing.

The Turning-Point

The kindness of Joseph von Spaun in providing Schubert for many years with manuscript paper has already been related.

He was untiring in his support and encouragement of the young composer. When Schubert was nineteen, Spaun wrote a delightful letter to Goethe, asking him to accept the dedication of eight small volumes of Schubert's songs, whose publication would be a 'beginning to his musical career.' Schubert's songs and numerous other compositions have, he says, already 'won the applause of strict judges of music as well as of music-lovers, of men as well as of women'; it is stressed that Goethe's magnificent poems are responsible not only for the existence of many of the songs, but also to an important extent for the composer's development as a song-writer; and finally, that the pianist who plays the songs to Goethe 'must not be wanting in skill and expression.' There came no answer. Goethe was doubtless overwhelmed with letters of this sort; his favourite composer was Zelter, who, when given a poem, first tried to conjure up a living picture of the situation, then read it aloud till he knew it by heart, and upon reciting it again found the melody came of its own accord. Goethe, at his age, could not be expected to reconcile himself to such music as 'Erlkönig,' which both in its substance and in the manner of its inception bore so strange a contrast to Zelter's gentleness and subordination.

In the same month as Spaun's letter, April, 1816, Schubert applied for a musical post at Laibach, but without success. He had, it is certain, fallen very much in love with a girl named Therese Grob, who had a lovely soprano voice and had two years previously sung the solo part of the Mass in F. She was not beautiful. 'But she was good,' Franz is supposed to have said, 'good to the heart. For three years I hoped to marry her, but could find no situation, which caused us great sorrow.'

Still more do these first attempts to win recognition and to obtain a settled job express a determination to follow the career of music, an intense and by now irresistible desire to escape from a household in which there reigned a perpetual atmosphere of schoolmastery and the most rigid paternal opposition to such a career.

Franz may have been persuaded to some extent by his new friends, Mayrhofer and Franz von Schober. It is also possible that he felt himself no longer in the same position in the second family, for his father had married again eleven months after the death of Elisabeth. There had been an addition of two daughters, now aged two and three respectively; and Ignaz, the eldest child, was forty-one when Anton, the nineteenth and last testimony to Franz Theodor's procreative energy, was born in 1826. It is hardly surprising that the latter kept a family register of such occurrences.

We may, in the cold language of the conscription papers of 1818, catch a glimpse of the Schubert sons. Ignaz, schoolmaster, is 'hunchbacked'; Ferdinand and Carl are both married, the former a schoolmaster, Carl a landscape painter, and tall of stature. Franz is described as 'schwach,' which was the military term for 'thin'. His height is just under five feet two inches. He certainly increased in bulk afterwards, though Spaun says he was solidly built and by no means a 'lump of fat,' and that his very youthful friend Moritz von Schwind already surpassed him in circumference.

A change was encouraged by habits which became an integral part of Schubert's existence. We have reached the turning-point in his career, signalised by the first pianoforte sonatas and an end to prolific song-writing.

The three sonata periods, culminating in 1817, 1825 and 1828, represent a division that may, without vital modifications, be observed in Schubert's output as a whole. There was a new outburst in 1822, with 'Alfonso und Estrella,' the Mass in A flat, the 'Wanderer' fantasia and the 'Unfinished' symphony, and in 1824 began the last intense period of composition, culminating in 1828 when Schubert produced masterpiece after masterpiece at a dramatically forced tempo.

After 1817, the succession of musical events is, for a while, no longer an almost completely satisfying tale in itself. Five comparatively fallow years followed upon freedom.

Schubert and Vienna

Eduard von Bauernfeld, in a letter to a prospective biographer of Schubert, thirty years after the composer's death, declares that the only possibility lies in a kind of poetical description. Schubert would be astonished, it has been remarked, at the documents that have now been collected about his uneventful life; yet the above conception is not outworn. Failure to recognise Schubert's stature as a composer has been inflamed by the fanciful development of certain themes, all of them tending to an unserious view of his personality. He was, of all the great composers associated with Vienna, the only Viennese. His boyhood was spent in an atmosphere affected by the nobility of four of the greatest musicians the world has known; in a city, also, filled with popular music of all kinds. Vienna was, as Professor Dent has pointed out, the meeting-place of musicians from Italy, Hungary, Poland and Bohemia—all of them countries where there is a 'widespread primitive gift for singing and playing instruments.'

In Schubert's compositions there is a perfect fusion of popular and serious music (the gulf between the two at the present day is significant); we may discover in the C major symphony the characteristics of 'Bratl' music and of the calls of lavender-women, in a simple Ländler the boldness and force of the third movement in the D minor quartet.

There were other influences besides those of Gluck, Mozart, Haydn and Beethoven on the one hand, of marches and street songs on the other. In 1816–17 the operas of Rossini took Vienna by storm. 'L'Inganno Felice,' 'Tancredi,' 'L'Italiana in Algèri,' and later 'Elisabetta' and 'Otello' enjoyed a fabulous success. Of the last, Schubert wrote in 1819 to his friend Anselm Hüttenbrenner—'One cannot deny him [Rossini] extraordinary genius. The instrumentation is sometimes most original, the voice-part also, apart from the usual Italian gallopades and several reminiscences from "Tancredi."' A critic writing in 1824 about some recently published Schubert songs finds also in

'Wehmut' reminiscences of 'Tancredi'—the 'famous bass from the first finale, B♭ D F—B♭ E♭ G♭—B♭ D♭ F♭G♭—B♮ D♯ F♯, and so on, four or five times'—a progression he then suggests to pianoforte tuners as a test of cleanness.

It is difficult to estimate the influence of Rossini on Schubert, for music has not yet become, in such matters, a dependable prey to analysis. The C major symphony has been described as a conflict between Rossini and Beethoven, the change from minor to major at the beginning of the A minor quartet as typically Rossinian. But the side-by-sideness of suffering and ecstasy exists deep down in Schubert. The change of mode in the A minor quartet is not facile; the emotional effect is not in that, but in the ecstatic soaring upwards of the original theme. It is comparable with the miraculous changes in 'Auf dem Flusse,' in 'Der Wegweiser' and in 'Trockne Blumen.' They are made suddenly, without sophistication as in Chopin, for instance, and nothing in music is more deeply affecting.

The Italian influence may be seen unmistakably in certain works, in the marches (where the change of mode is facile, like Rossini's) and in the sixth symphony, or in the finale of the G major quartet. It is confined rather to procedures recommended by their temporary fascination for a city amorous of gaiety.

It is important to realise that Franz Theodor's stubbornness was dictated not only by his conception of music as a precarious means of existence, but also by his fear of the atmosphere into which his son, as a free artist, would be drawn. Franz's boyhood was lived under the shadow of invasions more portentous than that of Rossini. Dr. Reeve, an Englishman who was in Vienna during the first campaign of 'War and Peace,' has left a vivid picture of the conditions there. Politics were not discussed. No circulating libraries were allowed, no reading-rooms or clubs. There was the most rigid censorship of books and newspapers.

English papers, Dr. Reeve complains, stopped many days

at the Post Office to pass through this formality. The people were kept in ignorance. Amusement had become their only object. Shops closed early so that their owners might return to the suburbs in time to prepare themselves for the opera. 'The Viennese,' says Dr. Reeve, 'are never at home and alone.' There might be some occasional fantastic sign of war in the bodies of French soldiers floating down the Danube and said to have been drowned by the Russians; then, suddenly, Napoleon enters the city, subjecting it to untold hardship. The censorship was powerless against enlightenment of this kind. But professors who were so bold as to interest their pupils in Kant were dismissed. The Viennese did not, like the Fabians, have to 'stretch their foreheads like concertinas' in order to understand one another's small talk. Conversation at table, the English visitors tells us, was of lovers and diseases. The only adventures that were restricted were those of the mind.

It is difficult to exaggerate the significance of this. Schubert's quickness to absorb the past and present of Viennese music, its utmost perfection and rudest simplicity, his quickness to reflect the momentary triumph of a foreigner, finds only an apparent parallel in his reaction to Viennese life. We have seen that the Schuberts came of a stock most antipathetic to the looseness and gaiety of Vienna. Franz's attitude to life remained deeply earnest. But, though music was unhampered by the censorship, Schubert became intimately acquainted with men who were sharply affected by the narrowness of the State, and whose whole behaviour was expressive of violent protest. He himself wrote music for a libretto that had been already banned. 'Light head, light heart!' he wrote in his diary while still a schoolmaster; 'too light a head usually conceals too heavy a heart.' His youth was touched, midway, by tragedy. The fabric of his thought and feeling was darkened by an overwhelming despair, which found upon occasion an accompaniment of more than usually excessive lightheartedness. Schubert's life cannot be interpreted as a comfortable acceptance of Bohemianism and foolhardiness, but rather as a tragedy of exhaustion in conflict with the unlucky times and with the prevailing reckless conception of living.

The Circle

From his earliest days, friendship had been almost as necessary to Schubert as music itself. That he had a remarkable gift for making friends is certain.

'I need hardly tell you that with my natural frankness I get along very well with all these people,' he writes from Zseliz, after a lively description of everyone there, from the coachmen to the countess.

In those inexplicable years of miraculous creativeness and of constraint as a schoolmaster, Schubert began to gather round him a circle of young men who were attracted by the magic of his personality, and held together by it, though they were of the utmost diversity of character and aim.

In the hours spent with his friends Schubert found some compensation for the hard circumstances of his life, as well as some relaxation from work, in which he must have used himself up with fierce intensity. He was not happy in every kind of society. 'Schubert is much praised,' wrote Carl Beethoven, 'but is said to hide himself.' An explanation of this may be discovered in a passage from Franz von Schober's Memoirs: 'As much as Schubert liked to join the companionable circle of his friends and acquaintances, which he always enlivened with cheerfulness, wit, and a healthy judgment, so much did he dislike appearing in formal society, in which he earned for himself through his retiring and unobtrusive behaviour the quite undeserved opinion that his personality, apart from music, was altogether insignificant. If, unhappily, there chanced the opportunity to spend in an intimate circle an evening already promised to some such formal society, or if a lovely summer evening tempted him into the open air, Schubert was easily led to break his word, a thing that was often reckoned heavily against him, though it was the only kind of disloyalty of which he was capable.'

Schober, the most intimate of Schubert's friends (of which a delicate proof may be seen in his styling himself Schobert), was a brilliant, cultured and worldly-wise young man, resembling a little, perhaps, Handel's friend Mattheson. Bauernfeld, who first met him in 1825, comments in his diary on Schober's adventurous life, and of how he had just been for a time an actor (in Breslau) à la Wilhelm Meister. 'He is liked by women in spite of his rather crooked legs. . . . Moritz (Schwind) looks upon him as a god. I find him fairly human, but interesting.'   Schwind, whose correspondence with Schober is couched habitually in extravagant terms of affection and admiration, was not alone in his hero-worship. Schober was certainly a most persuasive talker.

In Bauernfeld's 'Parody on the Schubert Circle,' which was read on New Year's Eve, 1825, Schober, as Pantalon, decides that the innermost nature of life is in rest. He despises position and occupation; work, even the most intellectual, is unworthy of him. He will, in future, lie on his bed, his flower-bed, and, imitating the plants, keep before him only the eternal substance of man and woman, and in doing so lead life back to its pure, original condition. This philosophy is greeted by Harlequin (Schwind) as 'magnificent, godlike, superhuman.' Schober had bought the Lithographical Institute, founded by Count von Palffy, and came into contact with Schwind through a few small orders, one of them possibly in connection with six lithographs by Schwind to illustrate *Robinson Crusoe*. Schwind had been brought up in the oriental Greek colony of Vienna. He was brilliantly gifted, and entered the university at the age of fourteen. He sketched promiscuously, on books and walls and in illustration of letters, at an early age, but did not decide on painting as a career until about the time he met Schubert. His art was affected fundamentally by Schubert's music, in which he could find a depth of feeling and clarity of expression absent from contemporary painting. Many of his works perpetuate the Schubertians in a delightful manner. He had red cheeks (a family trait), deep-set dark-blue eyes, and a queer way of entering a room, always one foot and one side first, as if he were probing the ground.

If Schwind was the most distinguished painter, Bauernfeld and Mayrhofer were the circle's most distinguished men of letters. Bauernfeld was a schoolfellow of Schwind. He met Schubert in 1825. Schwind made him read some of his poems to Schubert, the two then played pianoforte duets and all three afterwards repaired to the Gasthaus, where the friendship was firmly cemented. Bauernfeld, like Mayrhofer and many other poets at that time, was a government official. He became a favourite among Viennese dramatists. He was associated with Schlegel and Tieck in the famous 1826 edition of Shakespeare's plays, translating the *Two Gentlemen of Verona*, *The Comedy of Errors*, *Troilus and Cressida*, *Henry VIII* and *Antony and Cleopatra*, and others in collaboration with Mayrhofer. His temper was robust, he wrote, in a single year, nine plays, and lived to the age of ninety. All this is in great contrast to Mayrhofer, who was a hypochondriac, a romantically unhappy product of the time. There were others. Spaun has been mentioned; Stadler, Holzapfel, Senn —old friends from the Konvikt days—even the renowned Grillparzer upon occasion, all used to join Bauernfeld, Schober and Mayrhofer in reading their poems to the circle. There was a 'reading society,' often mentioned with enthusiasm in Schubert's letters. Franz von Hartmann records over twenty meetings in the earlier part of 1828. Schober always read, apparently; the works of Tieck and Kleist predominate; once it is poems by Schober, also Heine's 'Reiseideen' (in which Hartmann finds 'much wit but a false tendency'), and Goethe's 'Pandora' and 'Faust,' which Schober read 'gloriously.' Kupelwieser, who taught Schwind for a while, drew. Above all, Schubert played his pianoforte works, or accompanied his songs. Wonderful evenings they must have been, in which Schubert scattered without stint the riches of his divinely musical mind. The Schubertiads, for such they were called, were commemorated often in verse and drawing; by Mayrhofer's 'Geheimnis,' for instance, which Schubert himself set to music, though with a different feeling certainly from Handel's when he set Cardinal Pamphilij's 'Hendel non può mia musa;' and by Schwind's drawing, in which Death and the Powers of Darkness kneel behind Schubert, admitting their impotence, Schubertiads and literary meetings were sometimes preceded, and almost invariably followed, by entertainments of a more comfortable and less inspiring kind. On only one occasion after the above mentioned readings of Kleist, Tieck and Goethe does the diarist not repair to some Gasthaus. He is home at 9.45. Often it is the early hours of the morning before the friends leave Bogner's Café, or the Schnecke or the Rebhuhn, and Schwind runs through the streets imitating the flight of a bird, or there has been a heavy fall of snow, and a fight begins, Spaun and Franz Hartmann against Fritz Hartmann, Schober and Schwind, Spaun defending himself magnificently with outspread umbrella while Schubert takes no part.

Towards Recognition

Though the circle enfolded many of the most talented artists in Vienna, they were, nearly all, too young, too poor and too much without influence to be able to crown with any material results their enthusiasm for Schubert and their conviction of his genius. It was Schober who, after some difficulty, managed to persuade Michael Vogl to meet the young composer and hear some of his songs. Vogl was one of the most famous singers of the time; Schubert, when Spaun used to take him to the opera already as a pupil at the Konvikt, had worshipped him from afar, above all in Gluck's 'Iphigenia in Tauris.' The story of the meeting is familiar, of Vogl's telling Schubert there was stuff in him, but that he was too little of an actor and not enough of a charlatan. Schober says in his Memoirs: 'A partnership between the two artists, which grew more and more close, until death broke it, followed upon their first coming together. Vogl opened to his friend with well-meant advice the rich treasure of his experience, cared in a fatherly way for the satisfaction of his needs, for which his income from compositions was at that time insufficient, and prepared the way to fame through his magnificent interpretation of the songs.' Vogl took Schubert with him on visits to the Salzkammergut and Upper Austria. They were fêted everywhere. Schubert writes to his brother Ferdinand: 'The way Vogl sings and I accompany him, so that we seem to be fused for a moment into a single being, is something entirely new and unknown to these people.' In addition to Vogl's propaganda, help, and encouragement, one or two critics, Baron von Schlechta, for instance, were writing conscientious, appreciative and intelligent articles on Schubert's music, and the young composer was being introduced to influential families, the Fröhlichs and the Sonnleithners and many others.

'The Friends of Music'

Leopold von Sonnleithner had played an active part when, in 1812, the 'Society of Friends of Music' was founded. There were then over four hundred members, who belonged nearly all to the upper bourgeoisie; thirty years previously such a society would have been unthinkable. The 'concerts of the nobility' had ceased in 1808. Schubert as a boy had taken part in chamber music at home with his father and brothers, somewhat in the manner of the Bach family. There were countless circles of this kind in Vienna. The Schuberts themselves were always moving from house to house in order to accommodate an ever-increasing number of players, and the need for a concentration of forces was strongly felt. Within the 'Friends of Music' a series of concerts called 'Private

Abendunterhaltungen' were presently begun; their object was
to 'enliven members with music and decent conversation.'
On 25th January, 1821, Gymnich, a talented amateur,
sang Schubert's 'Erlkönig,' and thereafter Schubert's name
appeared frequently on the programmes. One Herr von
Jenger was commissioned by the society to write a biography
of Schubert, though after the appointed three months the
manuscript was still 'owing.' In 1826 Schubert was given
100 gulden; he had just dedicated his sixth symphony, in C,
to the society, but it was not performed until a month after his
death; the great C major symphony had to wait until 1850
to be given in its entirety at a society concert, though in 1839
two movements were played, separated by a Donizetti aria.
Schubert's music, apart from his songs, was hardly recognised.
It must be remembered that there were only seven years
between the publication—by private subscription—of Schubert's first works and his death; by which time about 180
songs had been printed, nearly all of them magnificent,
though there appeared soon afterwards many that Schubert
himself might have made no attempt to publish; in addition,
many valses, marches and four-handed works, but only three
pianoforte sonatas and one string quartet (in A minor), and
no symphonies or dramatic works whatever. Some of his
greatest works were not published until after 1850. The
existence of the 'Society of Friends of Music' was significant
of deep changes in Vienna, and the situation was aggravated
for Schubert by his dislike of high society, his inability to
reconcile 'town-bred politeness and human sincerity.' His
hardship was founded on this, that he was without patronage
—the exception will appear shortly—and could not possibly
live on the income brought in by his compositions. With
the exception of two opus numbers, all Schubert's works up
to the time of his death were published by Viennese firms;
and these, headed by Diabelli, offered him terms—even when
they themselves approached him—that were inhuman.
Schubert had also no instinct for his own advantage. He sold

Diabelli the rights of eighteen volume of songs for 800 florins; he wrote to Goethe in 1825, and sent him songs which a non-musician was not likely to appreciate; he dedicated to Beethoven nothing more representative of his genius than the E minor variations, op. 10—though this may have been because it was the only serious instrumental work he could get published at that time (1822).

Schubert was always anxious to obtain a definite and continuous job, in order to secure himself against a too oppressive poverty. He went in 1818 to Zseliz in Hungary, as music teacher to Count Esterházy's children. There he lived with the servants, wrote some vigorous and interesting letters, received two gulden per lesson, and, if not then, on his second visit in 1824, became enamoured of the count's younger daughter, Caroline.

Illness and Death

That so little is definitely known about Schubert's romances has frequently inspired novelists and playwrights to adventurous and picturesque theories. Even the best of Schubertian plays, by Carl Costa, has for its central theme a clearly unhistorical feminine rivalry for the hand of the composer. The prevailing uncertainty on these matters is due probably less to any clever concealment on Schubert's part than to his lack of recognition during his lifetime.

His letters were not jealously saved; of his diary, only extracts from eleven days remain; the others were sold by an antiquarian leaf by leaf as curiosities. Beethoven's last doctor left a convincing account of the musician's final illness; but in Schubert's case there is scarcely any evidence of treatment.

That his youth was touched by tragedy we have said, tragedy which plunged him from time to time in immeasurable grief. In 1824 he writes to Kupelwieser: 'Picture to yourself someone whose health is permanently injured . . . ;

picture to yourself, I say, someone whose most brilliant hopes
have come to nothing, someone to whom love and friendship
are at most a source of bitterness, someone whose inspiration
. . . for all that is beautiful threatens to fail, and then ask
yourself if that is not a wretched and unhappy being.' His
illness, the responsibility for which has often been ascribed to
Schober, marks properly a division in his life. He was a
patient at the Vienna General Hospital at the beginning of
1823, where, in intense physical pain, he composed 'Die
Schöne Müllerin.' It is not absolutely certain that Schubert
had contracted venereal disease. Bauernfeld's remark that
'Schubert is half-ill; he needs young peacocks, like Benvenuto
Cellini' need signify very little, as a reference to the passage
in the Memoirs will show. The suggestive facts are not this,
or Schubert's having for a time to wear a wig, but the length
of the illness in which loss of hair was only an incident, and
its intermittent nature and possibly the failure of his friends to
mention it by name. Early in 1824 Schubert is found fasting
for a fortnight—though fasting, it seems, was a treatment
prescribed for any chronic illness—a little later he begins a
new course of diet and baths; in April, his left arm is hurting
and he cannot play the piano at all. Then, for a year and a
half, he is apparently well; but there comes another attack in
the form of frequent and terrible headaches. He was exhaust-
ing himself, moreover, in a last dramatic outburst of composition. Spaun says that 'no one who ever saw him at his
morning's work, glowing and his eyes aflame, even with a
changed speech . . . will ever forget it. . . . I hold it beyond
question that the excitement in which he composed his finest
songs, the "Winterreise" in particular, brought about his
untimely death.'

In October, 1828, Schubert went to live with his brother
Ferdinand in the rural suburb of Neue Wieden; on the last
day of the month he was having supper at a tavern when
suddenly he started up after a mouthful of fish and said he
had been poisoned. On 12th November he wrote to

Schober: 'I am ill. I have had nothing to eat or drink for eleven days, and can only stagger, exhausted, between chair and bed. . . . If I eat any food at all, I cannot keep it down. Come to my rescue in this desperate condition with something to read.' He has read four novels by Fenimore Cooper, and asks for another, should Schober have one.

The length and progress of the illness correspond with that of a virulent attack of abdominal typhoid, which, owing to unhygienic conditions, was a very common disease at that time in Vienna. It had no connection with the illness whose course we followed previously.* Schubert fell into a delirium. He thought he was being buried alive. Ferdinand tried to persuade him that he was in his own room and lying on his own bed. 'No, it is not true,' was the answer, 'Beethoven is not lying here.' In the afternoon of 19th November, Franz Schubert died.

'The last master of Song has passed away,' wrote Grillparzer in his funeral oration for Beethoven.

As Anschütz read the words on that famous occasion, Schubert stood at his elbow. After the ceremony, Schubert and some friends drank to him who should most quickly follow Beethoven. On the anniversary of this momentous day there was given a public concert of Schubert's works, from which he gained £32. It was the first and the last.

A bundle of his manuscripts, among which must have been some of the greatest music the world has known, was valued at 8s. 6d.

Evaluation

A man who may be dismissed with anecdotes, a composer without intellect or even consistency of ideal and experiment, whose creations were unconscious and hardly understood by himself; such has been the common conception of Schubert.

* See detailed article by Dr. Schweisheimer in the *Zeitschrift für Musikwissenschaft* (Leipzig).

That it was so in the very beginning may be seen from a letter of Anton Ottenwald, written just after he had made Schubert's acquaintance at Linz in 1825, in which he tries to reconcile Schubert's discourse 'on art and poetry . . . and on the relation of the ideal to life' with all he had heard of his way of composing. Ottenwald expresses his increasing astonishment at each fresh proof of a profound mentality.

The musicians in Schubert's circle were tragically blind to his greatness. Max Friedländer relates how Franz Lachner, a well-known contemporary and friend of Schubert, said to him as an old man: 'It's a pity Schubert did not learn as much as I did; otherwise, with his extraordinary talent, he would *also* have become a master'; while Randhartinger, who was at school with Schubert, declared himself 'sorry that his friend remained until the last a bit of a dilettante.' These ideas have persisted. Busoni called Schubert a talented dilettante; others have contented themselves with a description of his music as 'adipose tissue.'

Yet this is the Schubert we have observed, at the age of fourteen, modelling himself energetically on Zumsteeg's ballads; perfecting his mastery in two hundred songs before the 'Erlkönig,' his opus 1; who copied out the full score of the minuet in the 'Jupiter' symphony; and acquired practical experience and the widest knowledge of Viennese classical music as a choirboy and violinist for five years at the Imperial Konvikt. It is the Schubert who composed two symphonies, one of such infinite poetry, poignancy and colour, and so perfectly expressed, that it has won deeper affection than any other work of its kind; the other so tremendous in idea, of such power and exhilaration, that only the greatest Beethoven may be played directly after and not lose significance for the excited imagination. It is the Schubert of the string quartets in A minor, D minor and G, and of the unapproachable quintet in C; of the seventeen pianoforte sonatas and of nearly four hundred pages of pianoforte duets, among them such wonderful works as the fantasie in F minor, the grand duo in

C, and 'Lebensstürme.' In all these branches of composition Schubert created works that have not since been surpassed. In another, that of song, he is quite unequalled among all the composers.

'To make an epoch in the world,' says Goethe, 'two conditions are notoriously necessary—a good head and a great inheritance.' Schubert had a magnificent inheritance, the dawn of German lyrical poetry and its timely perfection in Goethe; which circumstance (granted his peculiar gifts) determined the flavour and magnitude of his achievement as certainly as did the French Revolution that of Napoleon and the darkness of the Popes that of Luther. Schubert had a finer appreciation of poetry than his predecessors. His general culture was not in such stark contrast to his musicianship as has often been supposed.

He responded unfailingly to great poetry, but was also quick to seize upon some picturesque detail or situation in a poem of secondary significance, should it provide a fine musical possibility. Already at the age of seventeen Schubert's vision had a marvellous quality which enabled him to reach the universal through the particular. A conception of 'the endless and incommensurable' was not necessary to him. His invention in the songs is absolutely inexhaustible. Not only has he a unique power of evoking in the very first bars of a song the poetic atmosphere of his subject, there is also unending resource in the balance and colour of modulations, in enlarging or condensing phrases and compensating this through variations in melody or rhythm, until everything is of the greatest liveliness and plasticity.

When we turn to the man, it is to be astounded at the physical feat represented by the enormous amount of music he composed in seventeen years. His letters from Zseliz and on his journeys with Vogl reveal not only poetical appreciation of the scenery but a lively gift of characterisation, a robust way of thinking and observation of minute details. Schubert the child of Vienna, the disappointed lover and downtrodden musician is too comfortable a conception. His modesty and simplicity have led to underestimation of his character.

We have seen his attitude to Rossini; how different was that of Berlioz, who on meeting a Rossini enthusiast 'eyed him with a Shylockian scowl' and growled between his teeth, 'Miscreant! would that I might impale thee on a red-hot iron.'

Schubert's was a simple, outwardly uneventful life, without hatreds or intrigues, without dramatic triumphs or defeats, without fame or fortune or momentous journeys. Inwardly, the scene is of untold warmth and richness. Life and music share most, perhaps, that dual quality whose effect Dvořák, with just emphasis, likened to that of 'gathering clouds, with constant glimpses of sunshine breaking through them.'

BIBLIOGRAPHY

Bericht über den Internationalen Kongress für Schubert-forschung. (Augsburg, 1929.)

CAPELL, RICHARD: *Schubert's Songs.* 5s. (Benn, 1928.)

DAHMS, WALTER: *Schubert.* (Berlin, 1923.)

DEUTSCH, OTTO: *Franz Schubert. Die Dokumente seines Lebens und Schaffens.* (Munich and Leipzig, 1914.)

DEUTSCH, OTTO: *Franz Schubert's Letters and Other Writings.* Translated by V. SAVILE. O.P. (Faber, 1928.)

FLOWER, NEWMAN: *Franz Schubert, the Man and his Circle.* O.P. (Cassell, 1928.)

KOBALD, KARL: *Franz Schubert und seine Zeit.* (Vienna, 1928.) English Edition translated by B. MARSHALL.

KÖLTZSCH, HANS: *Franz Schubert in seinen Klaviersonaten.* (Leipzig, 1927.)

KREISSLE: *The Life of Franz Schubert.* Translated by A. D. COLERIDGE. 2 vols. O.P. (Longmans, 1869.)

TOVEY, DONALD F.: 'Schubert' in *The Heritage of Music,* Vol. I. Edited by HUBERT FOSS. 7s. 6d. (Oxford University Press, 1934.)

ROBERT ALEXANDER
SCHUMANN

BORN 8 June 1810   DIED 29 July 1856

By A. E. F. Dickinson

The Romantic Temper

Many creative artists are uncommunicative outside their art.
Of Handel and Bach, who tell us so much about themselves
in their music, there is not much else to learn except the
particulars of their changing environment. Perhaps it was
inevitable that the *élan vital* should be lacking from other
channels of self-expression, such as letter-writing or what we
may call musical agitation. The romantic movement
changed this relation of art and life. The workaday crafts-
man yielded to the self-exploring and self-conscious artist.
Beethoven's drawing-room successes did not blind him to the
essential unresponsiveness of his patrons, on which subject
he wrote and acted characteristically. But in his case this
constant embitterment at an unheeding world was too
accidental to detract from his artistic integrity.

Sensitive from the first, Robert Schumann soon proved an
out-and-out romanticist, increasingly conscious of a musical
mission to a philistine world, and interested alike in every
rapture of self-development and every pain of social frustration. As a composer he started by writing lyrical ballads,
followed by symphonies and music-dramas more lyrical
than architectonic. Literary leanings, a lack of Beethoven's
more concentrated creative urge and a certain didactic strain
bent his activity also to a long bout of musical journalism.

This continuous thought about music and musical opinion naturally overflowed into many characteristic letters. Schumann's music thus provides the supreme and abiding landmarks in a sentimental journey of musical endeavour, of which he himself has significantly supplied the supporting details.

Schumann had, however, an essentially retiring disposition. He was shy both about his music and in it, and in society his long silences, not only (like Beethoven) before strangers but before friends, were a continuous hindrance to his effective influence. We receive a constant impression of an escape from the world into the inarticulate unresolved moodiness of an eccentric personality. It is thus often necessary to guess at the real psychological factors behind the conventional gestures of expression, alike in the 'life' and in the music.

The Three Periods

Schumann's life may be divided into three main periods. His first twenty years were spent chiefly at his home at Zwickau and ended with two years at the university. Then came the important fourteen years at Leipzig. Schumann was now the avowed musician, and his common round of interest centred about his own creative activity, the *New Music Journal* and Clara Wieck, whom he married in 1840. Fina lly there were six years at Dresden, four years as conductor at Düsseldorf, and two in an asylum at Endenich.

Schumann's musical progress begins with the production of most of his piano music (1830–40) and of most of his songs (1840). The next four years show a stage of orderly instrumental expansion. The remaining period presents music of every kind. The years 1830, 1840, and 1844 thus appear as the turning-points of both his life and his art. In 1830 he began at last his desired career. In 1840 he attained to married happiness and a new release of creative spirit. By 1844 he had reached a developed maturity, from which he might conceivably have climbed to supreme heights, had not antipathetic surroundings and increasing mental derangement combined to distract him from his proper musical growth and ultimately to arrest it altogether.

Early Life

It is tempting to guess at Robert's chances of heredity. His father August, a clergyman's son, was sent away to school but was soon destined for the grocery business. The early influence of an uncle led him towards poetry and philosophy, and after settling down as a married grocer he fled into the book business, in which he had already snatched considerable experience. By the end of his sadly overworked and dyspeptic life he had written much and published a pocket World's Classics series and his own translations of Scott and Byron. He combined a capacity for hard work with considerable speculative enterprise, and cultured tastes with a notable desire to spread the literary gospel. Robert was less fortunate in his mother, a sentimental woman with passionate outbursts of visionary fervour which impressed Robert unduly. She opposed his hankering for such a precarious career as music, but she made up for it by gratifying almost every other wish. His letters to her indicate her gloomy, introspective outlook. Robert was the fifth child. None of the children reached fifty, and Emilie, the fourth, died in her twentieth year of a nervous disease. It was not a very healthy family.

Robert was sent to school at six and at ten passed on to the Lyceum of about 200 boys, where he spent eight years. He did reasonably well in class, aided no doubt by fatherly encouragement, and being at a day-school he was spared the early nervous strain which would certainly have overtaken him in the closer social proximities of a boarding school. He founded a school literary society and conceived a liking for Homer, Sophocles, Tacitus, and the then popular Jean Paul, whose highly strung emotionalism became a permanent influence. Meanwhile a limited but energetic town musician named Kuntzsch taught him music. His early performances included piano-duet arrangements of Haydn, Mozart and Beethoven symphonies (happy beginnings), ingenious extemporisations in illustration of local personalities, and the direction of a small band of eight. Schumann also heard much classical chamber-music (then a rare experience) at the house of a keen amateur, Carus, whose nephew's wife, Agnes, became one of the composer's many musical intimates. Choral concerts at Zwickau appear to have been rare, but there was plenty of well organised orchestral and band music, and the operas included 'Don Giovanni' and 'Der Freischutz.'

Schumann was fortunate enough to be taken at the age of nine to hear the great pianist Moscheles at Carlsbad. Clearly young Robert's music occupied the serious attention of his father, in spite of the mother's opposition. August must have remembered acutely his own early cultural ambitions. But he died in 1826, leaving the mother free to thwart at her will; two years later Robert was sent to Leipzig University to study law. He was now beginning to show the ready self-indulgences of a spoilt child, including a rather highfalutin taste for pretty girls, champagne and a generally higher standard of comfort than his allowance permitted. He expected his mother to pay up.

At the University

On leaving school, Schumann meditated in this strain:

'Now the inner man must come forth and show what he is: thrust out into existence, flung into the world's night, without guide, teacher and father—here I stand, and yet the whole world never appeared to me in a lovelier light than now as I confront it and, rejoicing and free, smile at its storms.' (Translation by Niecks.)

Like many other testimonials this is distinguished partly by what it does *not* contain—for example, a resolution to settle down and study law. The next two years proved how ineffective Schumann could be without his father at hand as guide, friend and in the best sense father. He started by going off with a newly found kindred spirit and Jean Paul lover, Gisbert Rosen, a law student who was quitting Leipzig for Heidelberg. He enjoyed in this way a congenial tour of Bayreuth, Nuremberg, Augsburg and Munich. At Augsburg he stayed with a Dr. von Kurer, through whom he met Heine at Munich. Schumann also developed a passion for Clara von Kurer which was sufficiently romantic not to cause any friction with her fiancé or any lasting regrets afterwards. His affection for Rosen was deeper and may have strengthened a previous hankering for Heidelberg.

Meanwhile there was jurisprudence at Leipzig. In compensation Schumann practised chamber-music with Agnes Carus and at the Wiecks'. Wieck was his piano teacher, a man of fierce and advanced ideals, as Schumann's biographer Niecks shows. Wieck held decided views about piano-teaching and his own capacity to teach, but he was systematic rather than pedantic, and his empirical principles sprang from musical impulses and considerable teaching experience, and were suitably modified for individual pupils. He welcomed virtuosity when it appeared—Clara, aged nine, was already showing it—but he also believed that the piano must sing. Schumann was a disputatious and forgetful pupil but he must have absorbed much sound principle and practical knowledge. In addition Wiedebein, a minor composer, gave him some useful advice on song-writing. The Gewandhaus orchestral concerts impressed Schumann and account, perhaps, for the contrasts that permeate his piano music. These musical recreations were his chief outlet, not undergraduate life, which disappointed him by its coarse heartiness. As it was, he was already complaining of constantly needing cheering up.

In 1829 Schumann migrated to Heidelberg. He now

enjoyed a richer social career, with Rosen and others as the permanent figures in a continually changing circle; and in Professor Thibaut he found both a vivacious lecturer and a sympathetic musician of the cheerfully limited type. He also heard Paganini twice at Frankfurt, an event which is recorded in some piano arrangements. Another thrill was Pasta's singing at the Scala, Milan, visited during a tour of Switzerland and Northern Italy. But Schumann's reports of the slovenliness both of Italian performances and of Heidelberg pianists suggest a critical standard; and his much applauded virtuosity at a Heidelberg concert must have been a challenging record of his increasing musical accomplishment.

After another year of intellectual dallying his musical genius took the offensive. Legal ambitions were easily crushed. After a twenty years' struggle 'between poetry and prose' (as he put it) what romanticist could doubt which was the aggressor? So he wrote to his mother, emphasising the call of genius, his determination to work hard and the awfulness of the alternative: finally he invoked Wieck for confirmation. Wieck's sublime confidence in his own teaching powers left him in no doubt about Schumann's potential virtuosity under his guidance, but he naturally questioned Schumann's will to make good and proposed a six months' trial. Schumann was ready to accept anything, so long as it was to be music there and then. But this struggle left him limp. After a month's dawdling at Heidelberg, he went on a pleasure trip *en route* for Leipzig. His first letter home frankly confesses his intellectual apathy. How very reassuring for Frau Schumann! Yet there is no greater testimony to Schumann's natural musical genius than this gauging within himself of depths as yet unplumbed. As a composer he had written some of 'Papillons' and the 'Abegg Variations,' all pieces of brilliant individuality (as Grillparzer noted in a Vienna paper) but scarcely a foretaste of later developments. Thus signally does a categorical 'Know thyself!' attend every nascent individuality.

Music at Last—Exit the Virtuoso

Schumann at first lodged with Wieck, who had now married again, and here, surely, there was every inducement to settle down. But he wanted to be everything at once, pianist, conductor and composer for a start. The reckless and secret adoption of a finger-adjuster of his own devising (after chafing at the slow progress of the first two years) ruled out once and for all the possibilities of piano virtuosity. After over a year of varied treatment of a dislocated third finger, Schumann had in 1833 to face the fact that he could never be a concert-pianist, never even the best player of his own piano works. Apart from the dissipation of talent which was certain to prevail in such a wayward nature, the career of a concert-pianist needed sterner stuff than Schumann was made of. We may cheerfully consider the disappointments he was saved as well as the creative happiness to which he instinctively and successfully turned. His pain at not being able to interpret his music himself was greatly to be alleviated by having a fine substitute in his own wife. There remains the possible disadvantage to his piano style that a lack of continued virtuoso-experience entailed. It is difficult to establish any facts in this matter.

The Leipzig Years

For composition Schumann had placed himself under Dorn, who was young, thorough and altogether a live wire. Schumann learnt the uses of fugue and the general value of reflection and method. He also studied lovingly Bach's *Preludes and Fugues* (Book I). It is interesting to read the romanticist's just tribute. 'Bach was a man; with him nothing is half done.' Yet he admired Jean Paul as fervently! The products of Schumann's own workshop were now beginning to accumulate. The piano music will be considered later. A symphony in G minor received public performance but has since never appeared.

During this fairly full creative period (1830–40) various events of personal importance occurred, and also the growth of a fresh undertaking, the editing of a new musical periodical. In 1833 Schumann was ill, and the deaths at the end of the year of his favourite brother Julius and sister-in-law Rosalie aggravated his melancholic condition. He begged his mother not to refer to these bereavements! One wonders why Agnes Carus or some other suitable person could not induce Robert to pull himself together. But probably he was in too neurotic a condition to be cured except perhaps, by an expert mental healer. (He had got thoroughly 'worked up' over the cholera panic in 1832 and the family anxiety about his excessive beer and cigars suggests that in his moods of depression he could not resist these indulgences.) It is not surprising that in this unhealthy state he turned for consolation to an uncritical, warm-hearted girl called Ernestine von Fricken, a resident pupil of Wieck. A year before, he had likened Clara to a distant altar-piece, but she was only fourteen and was away in Dresden. The separation, however, proved almost as intolerable to him as to her. The discovery of Ernestine's illegitimacy decided him to break off the unhappy engagement. Clara's star was now in the ascendant. Ernestine's identity has been preserved in 'Carnaval' in the motto-theme of A-s-c-h, her native town, and in 'Estrella,' a revealing portrait; and her father gave Schumann the theme for the 'Études Symphoniques.' On the whole Niecks shows good ground for summarising this as an episode of errors, in which serious neurosis played a significant part. It is a little odd, then, that during these morbid years the new paper came to birth and a flourishing youth under Schumann's editorship. It may be said in his defence that he was not the first person or the last to be such an ardent social reformer that he had no time to shoulder family burdens; also, that the effort of starting and maintaining a new paper, however thrilling, left him in a dependent, impressionable state of mind in which to encounter Ernestine's physical vitality.

The 'New Music Journal'

The idea of a serious musical journal, for the purpose of combating the general mediocrity of the German musical atmosphere, arose in 1833. After continual meetings of the Group thus called into existence, plans were complete; Schumann had of course had publishing experience in his youth. At first there was a board of director-editors. Wieck appears to have been the presiding and protecting spirit, Schumann the anonymous editor-in-chief, and the other principals were Knorr, a teacher, and Schunke, a gifted pianist whose initiation is romantically described in the *Journal*. In the background was, among others, Henriette Voigt, a charming personality to whose sensitive perceptions and musical household the *Journal* also pays happy tribute. In 1835, after nine months of twice-weekly publication, Schumann's editorship was openly declared. He carried on till 1844, defying all expectation. Ten years later he published a large selection of his own contributions, which includes the famous 'Hats off, gentlemen—a genius!' article (*Allgemeine Zeitung*, 1831) on Chopin's early Variations. In 1838 he went to Vienna with every intention of establishing the *Journal* there, but he found the atmosphere too reactionary. The *Carnival Jest* records this visit. Quarterly musical supplements began in 1838.

These ten years of disinterested musical propaganda—Schumann very rarely mentions his own works—are a remarkable chapter in musical history. Previously music criticism had either been fiercely analytical or fatuously eulogistic. The new *Journal*, while containing few of the theoretical essays promised in the prospectus, discussed new or forgotten musical developments with a composer's acuteness of ear, unwarped by a composer's prejudices, and with a dramatic vividness and a poetic touch that recall the dialogues of Plato. Never before or since has there been such a persistent attempt to greet personally the new generation and yet sift the good from the pleasing, finished work from laboured, art from virtuosity, genius from talent. The genius of German music has always been built up on a wide foundation of earnest experiment, and 1834–44 was, like our own time, a period of not easily scanned transition. Thus, at a time when originality was almost a crime, Schumann gave the steady support of his critical interest to newcomers: he secured many 'local correspondents.' Always whole-hearted in his favours, his perpetual panegyrics on Mendelssohn seem forced, but against these and other likeable adorations must be set the clairvoyant discoveries (from very early works) of Chopin and Brahms and the just recognition of the sheer magic of Berlioz and Wagner and the charming clarity of Bennett; as convincing fundamental hypotheses stand Schumann's rhapsodic but profound appreciations of the inexhaustible poet, Bach, of the Promethean Beethoven and of the 'everlasting youth' of Schubert, of whose C major symphony he proved the discoverer in every sense of the word. And his principal hate, Meyerbeer, was a perfectly reasonable one. Nor was our critic unmindful of performers: he gave virtuosity its due meed, and he recognised the importance of a 'preparatory school of public performance and concert routine,' such as the Euterpe Society at Leipzig provided. He also pleaded for a complete publication of Bach's works.

Apart from this steady construction of tested and working critical assumptions for the benefit of an ignorant and wayward public, the *Journal* introduces us to Schumann's 'romantic' bias for a concretely emotional interpretation and his derived interest in *harmonic* shades of meaning. But while he encourages general culture, he despises cheap literary comparisons, and insists on the widest possible aural training, such as can distinguish the trite melody of fashion from the deeper melodiousness of folk-song and the established masters. Sentence after sentence could profitably be learned and marked by performers, critics and audiences of to-day. And no editor was politer to his contributors.

This conscious movement to ring out the false was

dramatised by Schumann to himself as a league of spiritual personalities against the philistine confederacy of mediocrity and circus virtuosity. Somewhat in the same spirit, and after the manner of the Walt and Vult of Jean Paul's *Flegeljahre*, the editor often openly regards *himself* as a league of two complementary personalities, Florestan the ecstatic and Eusebius the sensitive, who also appear in odd superscriptions over some of the piano music. This division of the mind's response to art and life is useful when opinion has not grown to integral judgment (a distinction which the common dogmatism of to-day frequently obscures). It is also to be kept in mind in dealing with the elusive integrity of many pieces of Schumann's music. The first piano sonata is frankly 'by Florestan and Eusebius,' a quaint but accurate statement

Mendelssohn and his Circle

This regular work kept Schumann going in many ways being a realistic antidote to introspection as well as a basis of middle-class existence, and in 1835 a new stimulus arose in the arrival of Mendelssohn, fresh from triumphs at Düsseldorf, to conduct the Gewandhaus concerts. The relations of Schumann to Mendelssohn are somewhat obscure: after being friendly they became strained, anyhow on Mendelssohn's side. It is easy to see the attractions for Schumann of Mendelssohn's musical masterfulness as composer or conductor—a conductor who did something more than lead was rather a phenomenon at the time—and of his quick perceptions, wide culture and surface cordiality. It is less easy to understand how Schumann's adoration ignored Mendelssohn's smugness and 'push.' On the other side, while Mendelssohn's views on Schumann's amateurishness and journalistic tendencies are known to have been decidedly tart (in spite of all the admiration in and out of the *Journal*), a letter from Mendelssohn to Klingemann in 1847, which refers to malicious gossip attributed to Schumann, remains.

unexplained; and the omission of all reference to Schumann in the published Mendelssohn letters does nothing to remove the impression of a singular lack of generous impulses. There is no evidence of jealousy or party feeling on either side.

Another arrival, though a fleeting one, was Chopin. Wieck was elated, for here was Clara's opportunity. She played, besides two Chopin études, Schumann's first sonata. A month later she played the sonata to Moscheles. In the following year Ferdinand David arrived as leader of the orchestra and resident soloist. Schumann saw much of this fine musician later at the Leipzig conservatorium: they must have had much in common. Another newcomer in 1836 was Bennett, with whom Schumann enjoyed the most cordial relations, while retaining critical reservations as to the size of his creative genius. Bennett on his side was not more than politely impressed with Schumann's own music (up to that date), but he did much for it in England later, in happy recompense for the early interest taken in his own music by the *New Music Journal*. Frontiers were pleasantly forgotten.

Clara Wieck

Early in 1836 Schumann's mother died. He did not attend the funeral. The deepening intimacy between Clara and himself was now patent to all and now began the four years' painful struggle with her father, which in certain aspects of paternal obstinacy and egotism resembles the romance of Elizabeth Barrett and Robert Browning. On realising the changed situation, Wieck packed Clara off to Dresden. It is easy to understand his thoughts. Clara was now approaching the crisis of her career. What could upset things more than to allow her to tie herself up with the impecunious and intemperate Robert Schumann? That Clara could at the moment entertain other ideas of happiness than successful virtuosity scarcely occurred to him, for this crowning vicarious triumph had been his goal for years. When the now devoted couple continued to defy him, he brought Clara back to Leipzig, forbade her to see Robert, threatened him, and constructed round him a network of disapproval, slander and malice. A 'friend,' Carl Banck, furthered the cause of mutual mistrust.

A year later Clara played in public the first sonata, which Robert had dedicated and sent to her a year before. Music was the only crumb of love she could send him. He was at the concert, of course, and through a friend who was present they got into touch and on the next day became engaged. He wrote to Wieck to ask for his consent. Wieck became as offensive as ever, and later was slandering Clara as well as Robert. (It is not surprising that his first wife left him.) Meanwhile they had decided to force his consent by law. The question of Robert's temperance caused a serious check to the proceedings, but at last Wieck withdrew his objection and in September, 1840, they became united. (I have outlined the story as pieced together by Litzmann in his *Clara Schumann*.) Just before this, Schumann received news of the honorary doctorate conferred on him by the University of Jena, for which he had 'worked hard.' In this year, too, Liszt flashed into his acquaintance. 'Liszt's world is not mine,' he wrote.

Piano Music

We may now turn to the large body of piano music which Schumann had produced in the last ten years. Some of it is widely familiar to modern concert-audiences and needs no comment, but as Schumann himself observed even of his most popular and animated piece, 'Carnaval,'* his many subtleties of mood do not lend themselves to public presentation; and he was particularly fond of writing suites of delicately contrasted pieces. He is therefore chiefly for the private performer and

---

* On this see Browning, *Fifine at the Fair*, xc–xcii.

G

listener and, like Bach, demands the intimacy of 'music on the hearth.' There is much worth exploring, and Mr. Fuller Maitland's excellent pocket guide makes a detailed survey here superfluous. The 'Fantasia' (1836) and 'Humoreske' (1839) are the biggest creations, without possessing the calibre or cumulative power of a Beethoven sonata, and the earlier sonata No. 1 and 'Études Symphoniques' fall not far behind. The miniatures should not be neglected: 'Papillons,' the 'Intermezzi,' the 'Davidsbündlertänze,' and the later 'Bunte Blätter' and 'Albumblätter.'

A deeper note, reflecting the passionate struggle of 1836–40, underlies the 'Fantasiestücke,' 'Kinderscenen,' 'Kreisleriana' (a romantic greeting both to Clara and to Hoffmann), 'Novelletten' and 'Nachtstücke.' Many of the individual numbers of these sets are highly developed entities. From the simplest (such as the beautiful epilogue to the 'Kinderscenen') to the most elaborate or fanciful, they present something so genuine and sensitive that their friendly reception into all musical circles is assured. Well might Schumann feel more than a journalist.

Songs

Up to now Schumann had, in spite of Schubert's signal example, a prejudice against song-writing. In 1840 songs began to come and it ended in being a song year. The dictum 'What Schubert was to Goethe, Schumann was to Heine' must be challenged. Schumann's songs do not attract, like Schubert's, by their abundant musical flow from their poetic source, but rather by their fitness to given poetry, as in the exquisite restraint of 'Ich hab' im Traum geweinet.' Their appeal thus centres round a particular taste for the German romantics. Within these limits the songs include many fine and distinctive examples. Two sets, the 'Dichterliebe' and 'Frauenliebe und Leben,' contain the most complete expression of Schumann's glowing romantic sympathies, but one must not forget the more isolated ecstasies of 'Frühlings-nacht' and 'Mondnacht,' and the dramatic power of ballads like 'Belzatsar,' 'Der Schatzgräber,' and the popular 'The Two Grenadiers.' It will be noted that, like the orchestra in Wagner, the piano offers usually the chief comment and always 'the last, the parting word.'

Robert and Clara

Meanwhile the man and the woman, the creative composer-journalist and the humble executant, were settling down. Fortunately Clara was of the admiring kind and was prepared to stop practising if it interfered with Robert's composing, although she realised that they could ill afford to let her wait on opportunity. (Daughters were born in 1841 and 1843.) Something of the ins and outs of this problem and of other close relations is recorded in the diary which they kept for three years, each writing nominally in alternate weeks. We can there observe their pilgrimages through the '48' and Beethoven symphonies, played from score, as well as the shared raptures over new works, and worries over the demands of the 'beastly' paper, regular and not too lucrative. Clara had long kept a diary.

In 1843 the Leipzig conservatorium was founded by Mendelssohn after much negotiation, and Schumann obtained on the staff a post for piano and composition. This engagement was interrupted by a Russian concert tour with Clara in 1844, followed by a breakdown in health and departure to Dresden, but the loss of so absent-minded and ineffective a teacher as Schumann cannot have been widely felt.

First Orchestral Works and Chamber-music

During these last four years Schumann was expanding rapidly as a composer. He advanced into orchestral, chamber, and dramatic-choral music, and his powers noticeably matured in the process. In 1841 came two symphonies, separated by a symphony without slow movement whose-complex title 'Overture, Scherzo and Finale' has perhaps contributed to its undue neglect. The latter was followed by a fantasia which we now know as the opening of the piano concerto. Another symphony was sketched but went no further. The first symphony in B flat, originally conceived as a spring symphony (with titles to each movement), echoes Beethoven's lyrical B flat masterpiece. The work is loosely constructed. Schumann's themes often begin well but do not lead to anything in particular, so that they make a fussy show of individuality or are too quickly forgotten in a new subject. But with a sympathetic conductor, capable of integrating the straggling episodes and uncouth orchestration as well as of realising the ecstatic intention of the general conception, the symphony can make a striking public appearance, second only to Beethoven and Brahms in its century. Its cheerful tunefulness and generally original impulse triumphed over its awkwardness at the first performance, and secured its composer a wide interest that he had not enjoyed before. The second Symphony in D minor (now No. 4, owing to a late revision) is more deeply conceived, and has striking moments, such as the spacious opening, the incursion of the finale theme in the first movement, the main theme and violin arabesques of the romance, and the transition from the scherzo to the finale; and the use of a motto-theme and other gestures of connecting the movements is a notable approach to Wagnerian opera, even if as 'obvious' in execution as Franck's. The lack of a spontaneous expansion, inherent in the themes, remains. In the one-movement fantasia the piano is always at hand as announcer and illuminating commentator, so that despite orchestral jejuneness ('Chamber-music!' is one verdict) the development is well and truly planned. This movement is thus at once the pianist's joy, the public's favourite Schumannianum and the critical Schumannite's consolation.

In 1842 Schumann's initiative produced three string

quartets, a 'piano' quintet and piano quartet, and three pieces for piano trio. The quartets, like the symphonies, show a lack of string experience, or perhaps of sheer aural observation, such as he displayed so much as a teacher: there is too much cross-string writing, in unhappy imitation of pianistic arpeggios. These works carry Schumann's distinction without adding much to it and cannot be ranked with the Brahms and Franck quartets as in the authentic line of succession, except perhaps the A minor example. The quintet, on the other hand, is a masterpiece of music and of piano-string writing.

Oratorio

Next year, after an attack of nervous exhaustion that had obliged him to stop work, Schumann wrote the variations for two pianos, two 'cellos and horn, later to become the fine composition for pianos only, and the cantata 'Paradise and the Peri,' which is an oratorio in general structure, though scarcely in spirit. In spite of the composer's timidity at rehearsal—a quality which was to prove so fatal later—the work was well received and repeated with increased enthusiasm in a week. The plastic, sensuous metre and marked terseness of *Lalla Rookh*, from which the libretto was translated and adapted, makes good material for an elaborate setting, and the fanciful idealism appealed to Schumann. The oratorio, like all oratorios, is too long, and its shallow sentimentality (especially the glorification of a 'righteous war') and frequent invitations to exuberant bathos are all too readily accepted by the composer; and his vein of pious choral reflection suffers from Mendelssohn's facile graciousness of manner. These disbeliefs suspended, there are many striking touches and the lyrical tone of the whole is remarkably well sustained.

Departure to Dresden—Further Expansion

In 1844, after the Russian concert tour, Schumann decided

to place the *New Music Journal* in other hands. In August his health broke down and he went eventually to Dresden, where after a neurotic crisis he improved and later decided to settle. Too much thinking out music and thinking about music had jaded him, and in Dresden he enjoyed the sparser musical routine. But meanwhile a fresh phase of romantic idealism had gripped him in 'Faust.' This effort and certain tricks which his ear or brain now began to play him left him in a helpless, morbid state for most of 1845. The main distractions were the artistic figures whom Ferdinand Hiller gathered round him, including the painter Bendemann, best of friends, and that clever, 'mad,' loquacious Richard Wagner, who had sent his score of 'Tannhäuser.' It is not difficult to see why the reserved and disinterested Schumann did not incline to the flamboyant and egotistical Wagner or to the unabashed earthiness of his musical appeal, far-reaching as it might be. A further stimulus to energetic life was a new interest in counterpoint, which issued in the playful academicism of the canonical studies and more pleasing sketches for pedal piano and in the sextet of organ fugues on the theme B-A-C-H, the romanticist's 'Art of Fugue.' Finally, the orchestral fantasia expanded into the piano concerto, the breezy finale of which is Schumann's *L'allegro*. In the following year appeared another vigorous work, the C major symphony (No. 2), the moodiness of which reflected, as he explained later, his struggle with carnal apathy. The work is different from its predecessors without being an advance on them.

The year 1847, which began with the diversions of concert touring in Vienna and elsewhere, was a time of unusually varied creative activity, and included two good piano trios, many choral pieces and a start at an opera, 'Genoveva,' which was completed in 1848. A Schumann opera on a sensational story was something of a misfit and the composer's efforts to tone down the libretto did not help. Schumann had little of the dramatic virtuosity which animates a successful

opera, or of that command of generating *motif* which illumin-
ates the lightest Mozart and the heaviest Wagner: his was a
lyrical frame of musical ideas. Golo, that Iago-like figure,
is more like Werther at times! Yet 'Genoveva' contains
some splendid music, and as one of the early experiments in
romantic, German opera, as opposed to the 'canary music'
of Italy, it commands the historian's best attention.

Another undramatic work of 1848 was the music for
Byron's *Manfred*, which is best judged as a musical illustration
for the original, rather than as incidental stage music. We
can then appreciate without any feelings of inappropriateness
the first three and last numbers of Part II, and above all the
fine overture, whose yearning second subject reappears in
the Astarte scene.

Earlier in this 'the most fruitful year of my life' Schumann
took on Hiller's male choir (for a year) and founded a choral
union of his own, with Clara as accompanist. The latter
society, though dogged by Schumann's inarticulateness and
lack of command, was a thoroughly progressive, sociable
and spirited affair, as Niecks was able to learn from a member.
Bach, Handel, Palestrina, Mendelssohn and Schumann were
the chief composers. This regular choral experience and his
previous dramatic experiments enabled Schumann to complete 'Scenes from Faust.' Part III was performed on the
same day at Weimar, Leipzig and Dresden, at the celebration
of the Goethe centenary in 1849; the whole work was first
given in 1862. Starting with the final Transfiguration scene
(1844) Schumann warmed to Goethe's greater inspiration,
but in different stages and degrees. The ominous Part II is
the most interesting of the latter additions, the overture being
tired work. Part III is Schumann's greatest choral effort.
Its subject and mystical treatment suggest a comparison with
Brahms's 'Requiem' and 'The Dream of Gerontius.' After
these masterpieces of sheer music and intensely personal
emotion the gospel of the Ever-womanly sounds self-
conscious, diffuse and chorally academic or awkward. In

its own wayward and fanciful style the work is highly original
and sometimes great.

Schumann was no political agitator, and the Dresden
revolution of 1849 made him find a more secure bower of
the muses in a little village near Dresden. Here he continued
his silent existence in a lively household. There were now
five children, 'the wife, as of old, always striving onwards.'
Clara must certainly have had her share of striving. Fortunately she was encouraged by the healthy creativeness which
the Dresden move seemed to have facilitated. For the family
Robert had written the 'Album for the Young,' which is still
proving one of the best of its kind. He wrote during this
period (1848–50) the charming duets 'Bilder aus Osten',
notable choral works, 'Requiem for Mignon,' 'Nachtlied'
and the breezy 'New Year's Song'; attractive sets for vocal
ensembles; the lyrical 'cello concerto and a most eloquent
movement for piano and orchestra (op. 92); and solos for
oboe, clarinet and 'cello, all pleasantly typical.

The Appointment at Düsseldorf

During this time Schumann was agitating for a conductorship and in 1850 he obtained one at Düsseldorf through the
recommendation of Hiller, the out-going conductor. After
another concert-tour and the production of 'Genoveva' at
Leipzig the Schumanns moved. The new opportunities were
considerable and make one marvel at the German municipal
tradition in music. There was a regular and trained choir and
orchestra, well capable of performing new works, whether
Schumann's own or the young talent that he had always
sponsored and to which he now devoted an entire concert, an
honour without precedent. Behind this organisation was
the enthusiasm which Mendelssohn, Rietz and Hiller had
built up in turn by their energy and perseverance, and which
greeted the Schumanns with palms and hosannahs on their
arrival. The leader of the orchestra and a frequent visitor to

the house was Wasielewski, afterwards to become Schumann's biographer. There was also a capable musician named Tausch who acted as deputy-conductor from time to time.

The first season appeared to the Schumanns to have been a success, but there is much indirect evidence to the contrary. Schumann was far too absent-minded a conductor to gain the confidence of an orchestra, much less of a choir, and at rehearsals he was incredibly uncommunicative, uncommanding and unobservant. The musical or social irregularities which simply escaped his notice (not just his control) are the subject of many quite amusing tales, and he could not bear to be contradicted. He was, of course, quite unaware of his shortcomings and took cold offence at the want of respect which became open in the choir in the second season; he regarded it as mere philistinism. In 1852 he was again seriously ill. Tausch deputised capably and the desire for his permanent substitution became vocal; in 1853 he was put in charge of the choral practices. The discontent at Schumann's conducting continued, and the holding of the Lower Rhine festival at Düsseldorf did not help his supporters. A new eccentricity was that he imagined all *tempi* to be too fast. After much anxious discussion in the autumn the committee tactfully suggested that for the sake of his health Schumann should give up for a time the conducting of all but his own works, Tausch being willing to act as general substitute. Schumann's characteristic reply was to absent himself from the next rehearsal, and from that moment he ceased practically to be conductor. In his thorough account Niecks has shown that the committee acted most carefully and sympathetically in the whole matter, and that Tausch was quite unfairly regarded by the Schumanns as an intriguer.

Brahms and the End

At the height of this unpleasantness Schumann was visited by a young composer with an introduction from Joachim,

Johannes Brahms. Schumann at once saw, even in the immature work he had brought, the genius for which he had been looking, to crown the romantic aspirations of the period with classical dignity and orderliness. He wrote and told Joachim that this was 'he that should come,' and sent the *New Music Journal* an inspired prophecy on the 'deep song-melody' of the new composer. Later in 1853 the Schumanns had a successful tour in Holland and on his return Robert collected his critical writings for publication. Then came disintegration, attempted suicide by drowning, and two years in a private asylum, where the patient was visited by Brahms, Joachim and Wasielewski among others. The known details of this collapse may be interesting to the student of morbid psychology but are scarcely in place here. The main fact appears to have been that an increasing failure to adapt himself to his environment, and the resulting submission to all the melancholy of imagined frustration, combined with physical causes to unseat the will Schumann needed to endure life to the end.

At Düsseldorf, Schumann wrote the Rhenish symphony (No. 3 in E flat), a large, portentous work with a folk-tuneful scherzo; 'The Pilgrimage of the Rose' and other choral ballads; an indifferent Mass and Requiem, a Teutonic oratorio on Luther having failed to crystallise; the attractive Weber-like 'Braut von Messina' overture and three overtures into which pomp and circumstance enter as tritely as in 'Finlandia,' and after which the gloomy *innigkeit* of the two violin sonatas is a relief; the forcible 'Fantasiestücke' (op. 111) and well-knit fughettas for piano; and finally the thoughtful 'Morning Songs,' which brought the composer back to his starting-point, piano lyrics.

The Man and His Art

A sense of frustration haunted Schumann's existence, and accounts, perhaps, for the absent, introvert look that Niecks remembered and the portrait in Grove's *Dictionary* confirms. In society he was always going off in a huff; as conductor and teacher he was incapable of 'tackling' anybody; his critical work scarcely routed the philistines; even as a composer he could only feel himself a fore-runner, quite apart from the fact that in reputation he was chiefly Clara Schumann's musical husband. His romantic spirit remains: like Rousseau, 'Si je ne vaux pas mieux, je suis autre.' In these bleak days when even in art wit is preferred to earnest sentiment, herd feeling to original thought, might to right, quantity to quality, it is refreshing to turn to the enthusiastic and inquisitive pages of the *New Music Journal*, to the lyrical fervour of the symphonies, and to the unpretentious sincerity of a fanciful but consistent musical idealism. In any account of the wider growth of musical appreciation in the last hundred years an Englishman is proud to mention Parry and Holst, but in their eloquent and many-sided plea for a deeper reverence for the uses of music these pioneers were anticipated, first and foremost, by the life-work of Robert Schumann, whose devotion to the musical cause was the chief part of his religion.

BIBLIOGRAPHY

JANSEN, F. G.: *Die Davidsbündler*. (Leipzig, 1883.)

JANSEN, F. G.: *Robert Schumanns Briefe. Neue Folge*. (Leipzig, 1886.)

JANSEN, F. G.: *The Life of Robert Schumann told in his Letters*. Translated by MAY HERBERT. O.P. (Bentley, 1890.)

LITZMANN, BERTHOLD: *Clara Schumann; ein Künstlerleben nach Tagebüchern und Briefen*. 3 vols. (Leipzig, 1902, 1905, 1908.)

LITZMANN, BERTHOLD: *Clara Schumann; an Artist's Life*. Translated and abridged by GRACE E. HADOW. O.P. (Macmillan, 1913.)

MAITLAND, J. A. FULLER: *Schumann*. 2s. 6d. (Low, 'Great Composers' Series, 1928.)

NIECKS, FREDERICK: *Robert Schumann*. 10s. 6d. (Dent, 'International Library of Books on Music,' 1925.)

SCHUMANN, EUGENIE: *Robert Schumann; ein Lebensbild meines Vaters*. (Leipzig, 1931.)

SCHUMANN, ROBERT: *Music and Musicians* (collected criticisms). Translated by FANNY RAYMOND RITTER. First series 8s. 6d.; second series 10s. 6d. (Reeves, 1883.)

WASIELEWSKI, W. J. VON: *Robert Schumann; eine Biographie*. 3rd edition. (Bonn, 1880.)

CARL MARIA VON WEBER

BORN 18 December 1786   DIED 6 June 1826

By Edwin Evans

Origins

Like most occupational names, that of Weber (weaver) is
common enough all over Germany and Austria, but the
particular family of Webers from whom the composer was
descended were Catholic landowners of Lower Austria.   In
1622 the Emperor Ferdinand II bestowed the title of Freiherr
upon Johann Baptist Weber.   Little else is known of him, but
more concerning his younger brother, Joseph Franz Xaver
Weber, who had a small theatre and concert-room erected
on his estate, and thus qualified to become the direct ancestor
of the musical Webers.   But this splendour was short-lived.
The family estates were lost in the confusion of the Thirty
Years' War, and although in 1738 the title passed from the
elder to the younger branch, its bearers were then reduced
to accept service with more fortunate members of the landed
aristocracy, such as Freiherr von Schönau-Zella, the management of whose property near Freiburg im Breisgau (Baden)
was entrusted to Fridolin von Weber, who died in 1754.   Of
his two sons, the elder, another Fridolin, dropped the title,
whilst the younger, Franz Anton, retained it.   Both brothers
entered the service of Karl Theodor, Elector of the Palatinate,
at Mannheim, then one of the most important musical centres
of Germany.   Fridolin had four daughters, all of whom became noted singers, the most famous being Aloysia, the second.
Mozart, who visited Mannheim at that time, first courted
Aloysia.   However, he eventually married Constanze, the
third sister, but he wrote one great part and many arias for

his sister-in-law, who had meanwhile married an actor named Lange. Fired by the example of Mozart, Franz Anton, the other brother, cherished dreams of becoming the father of a musical prodigy, and placed his two sons by his first marriage with Haydn as pupils, but his ambition was not fulfilled in them, although they displayed some talent. When over fifty he married again, his bride being Genovefa von Brenner, a Viennese girl in her 'teens; on 18th December, 1786, she gave birth to Carl Maria von Weber, in whom the father's ambitious dreams were destined at last to be realised.

This Franz Anton appears to have been an aristocratic scallywag, or so we would judge him to-day, though some allowance must be made for the times in which he lived. In the service of Karl Theodor he had fought against Frederick the Great in the Seven Years' War, and was slightly wounded at Rossbach on the Saale in November, 1757, after which he was fortunate enough to step into the shoes of his recently deceased father-in-law as steward to the Elector Clement Augustus of Cologne. His luck however did not hold out under the Elector's successor and, having meanwhile squandered his first wife's fortune, he led a drifting life. For a time he found employment with Friedrich August, Bishop of Lübeck and Eutin, and was conductor of the town band at the latter place when Carl Maria was born there. But the following year he was again adrift as director of a strolling company. His second wife died at Salzburg in 1789 and on 19th January, 1799, he wrote to a friend that he had given up theatrical life and resumed his military rank, without pay. As he was then sixty-four the prospects of Major Franz Anton von Weber were not rosy.

Boyhood and Youth

Meanwhile he had taken in hand his son's musical training. Carl Maria was a sickly lad. He suffered from a disease of the hip-bone, was unable to walk until he was four years old, and was fated to limp for the rest of his life. Delicate as he was, he was taught to play the piano and to sing almost before he could speak. He was not at first a very promising pupil, and his elder brother Fritz is said to have declared that, whatever else he might become, he would never be a musician. But at the age of nine, during a stay at Hildburghausen, he had lessons from Johann Peter Heuschkel, oboist and organist in the Court Chapel, to whom in later life he acknowledged his deep indebtedness. His earliest known composition, an organ-piece on the chorale 'Vom Himmel Hoch,' dates from then. In the first half of 1789, when he was eleven, he had six months' tuition under Michael Haydn, the composer's younger and less famous brother. The autumn found the family at Munich, where he had lessons in piano-playing and composition from Johann Nepomuck Kalcher, the Court organist, and in singing from Wallishauser, who had Italianised his name into Valesi. Four years later he became a pupil of the Abbé Vogler, in Vienna, who launched him upon his official career by securing for him the appointment of conductor of the Opera at Breslau. This was in 1804, when he was seventeen. But if, officially, his career begins at this point, he was far from being a novice. Haphazard as his musical training had been, he had profited diligently by every opportunity of improving it. But most of all, the precarious existence of his father, harmful as it had been in most respects, had provided him with an admirable environment for the acquisition of empirical knowledge. He was already an experienced composer, and there was little he did not know concerning the stage and its musical requirements. Colloquially speaking, he knew every trick of the trade. From his earliest years he had constantly contributed to the family exchequer by writing to order all kinds of music. Most of these early compositions were burnt, including his first opera, 'The Power of Love and Wine,' written at Munich in 1799. Of another opera, 'The Dumb Girl of the Forest,' produced 24th November, 1800, at Freiburg in Saxony, only three unpublished fragments remain, though it was performed on several other stages. His third opera, 'Peter Schmoll and his Neighbours,' composed at Salzburg in 1802, has remained unpublished, but the overture, revised in 1807, appeared as Op. 8 with a dedication to King Jerome of Westphalia. A few unimportant works, variously dated from 1798 to 1804, have survived, the most characteristic being a part-song, 'Leis', wandeln wir, wie Geisterhauch,' published posthumously. Among these works there is, however, one which throws light upon a curious episode. It is a set of variations, Op. 2, dedicated to Kalcher and printed in 1800, by the composer. The previous year he had become acquainted with a strange erratic genius who, failing to find a publisher for his works, had sought a means of printing them himself. This was Aloys Senefelder, known to fame as the inventor of lithography. He took a fancy to young Weber, and initiated him to the art he had developed only three years before. The young composer was much attracted to lithography, and might even have made it his career. Happily for music, his father quarrelled with the inventor.

Breslau

Young Weber reached Breslau in June, 1804, and took up his new duties after the summer recess. His position there was from the first somewhat difficult. At the outset Joseph Schnabel, the deputy conductor, left the theatre, declining to serve under a lad not yet eighteen. J. G. Rhode, the managing director of the company that financed the theatre, took kindly to him at first and wrote the libretto of 'Rübezahl' for him to set. Not much has survived of this opera. It is not even known whether he completed it, but the overture was revised some years later under the title 'Ruler of the Spirits.' Another composition of this period is an overture on a Chinese theme, 'Lieu-Ye-Kin,' which he found in Rousseau's *Musical Dictionary*. This he remodelled in 1809 when writing incidental music to Schiller's version of Gozzi's 'Turandot,' under which title the overture has come down to us. Early in 1806 he met with a serious mishap. He accidentally drank some nitric acid which his father was using for experiments in etching. His singing voice was ruined and even his speaking voice suffered permanently. A little later his difficulties became such that he resigned his appointment in May 1806. His life in Breslau had been anything but happy. His salary was insufficient, he had his father to maintain and an ill-advised liaison ran him into heavy debts which took some years to clear. Fortunately, he found employment with Duke Eugen Friedrich of Wurtemberg, who maintained an orchestra at Carlsruhe in Silesia, for which the young composer wrote two symphonies. But those were troublous times. The war with France was draining the resources of Germany, and the Duke found himself compelled to give up his establishment. He recommended Weber to his two brothers, the King of Wurtemberg and Duke Ludwig, the latter of whom appointed him his private secretary. After a short concert tour he took up his new duties at Stuttgart on 1st August, 1807.

Stuttgart and Darmstadt

The newly created King Frederick of Wurtemberg was married to the English Princess Royal, Charlotte Matilda Augusta, daughter of George III. He was talented, but tyrannical, mean and unscrupulous, and fond of coarse jests at the expense of those who could not retaliate. His brother, Duke Ludwig, having failed to secure the throne of Poland, was entirely dependent upon him, and the secretary's duties were mainly concerned with obtaining funds in circumstances that were generally humiliating. The King's favourite was an adventurer named Dillen, who, from being a groom in the ducal stables, had risen by devious ways to be a minister of state. Weber found friends in Danzi, the conductor of the Royal Opera, and Lehr, the royal librarian, but surrounded as he was with temptations, it is not altogether surprising that he gave way to dissipation under the influence of Franz Carl Hiemer, a fascinating man of letters, who belonged to a club called 'Faust's Ride to Hell.' It was, however, Weber's father, the Major, then in his seventy-fifth year, who precipitated the catastrophe. At the end of 1809 the composer discovered to his dismay that the old reprobate had pocketed certain sums of money which the Duke had entrusted to his son for the purpose of paying off a mortgage on the Carlsruhe estate in Silesia. The son decided to shield his father and take the blame on himself. On 9th February, 1810, a body of police invaded the theatre during the rehearsal of Weber's new opera 'Silvana,' and marched the composer off to prison, his father being ordered not to leave their apartment. In due course the two Webers were escorted to the frontier in the most ignominious fashion and expelled from the kingdom. The exiles did not have to travel far. First at Mannheim and then at Darmstadt they found a hospitable refuge and Weber soon settled down again to serious work. At Darmstadt he met his former master, the Abbé Vogler, renewed acquaintance with his fellow pupil from Vienna, Johann Gänsbacher, and formed a friendship with another of Vogler's pupils, Jakob Meyer Beer, who was destined to win fame in later years as Giacomo Meyerbeer. To him is dedicated the well-known 'Momento Capriccioso' for piano which Weber had brought with him from Stuttgart. Otherwise the most important of the many compositions that originated there is the opera 'Silvana,' already mentioned. He rewrote a considerable portion of it and it was eventually produced at Frankfort on 10th September, 1810, the day of a sensational balloon ascent by the celebrated Mme Blanchard, which considerably reduced the numbers of the audience. The principal part in it was taken by a young singer, then in her eighteenth year, Caroline Brandt, who little knew that she was destined to become the composer's wife.

Munich—Berlin—Some Tours and Marriage

Early in 1811 Weber set out from Darmstadt, and in March he reached Munich, where he found favour with the Court. Here was produced, on 4th June, the one-act opera 'Abu Hassan,' dealing with the *Arabian Nights* story of Fatima and Hassan who, to escape from their creditors, pretend to be dead. The libretto was by Hiemer, and the opera was in reality a humorous satire on its impecunious author's difficulties at Stuttgart. It brought better luck, for the Grand Duke of Hesse, Ludwig I, to whom it is dedicated, sent Weber 440 florins, which was then a handsome sum. The merry little overture 'Alla Turca,' composed at Darmstadt on 12th January, 1811, is still popular. The success of the opera, however, was a chorus of creditors: 'Geld! Geld! Geld! Ich will nicht länger warten!' It was during the composition of this opera that Weber, whilst on a tour with a friend, came across Apel's volume of Ghost Stories, one of which, *Der Freischütz*, attracted his attention as a subject for an opera, though seven years were to elapse before he took it up again.

At Munich the composer formed a close friendship with Heinrich Joseph Bärmann, the greatest clarinet-player of his day, for whom he wrote several works, and with whom he continued his tour. During their progress, Weber inadvertently entered Wurtemberg, and was placed under arrest, but as the frontier to which he was conducted lay in the direction of his journey, he suffered nothing worse than a 'lift' on his way. After they had visited Prague, Dresden and Leipzig, they accepted an invitation from that eccentric prince, Duke Emil Leopold August of Saxe-Gotha, whose hobby was to appear in female attire, and who wore every day a differently coloured wig. Spohr was then his Kapellmeister and was not overjoyed at meeting again with Weber, of whose way of living he had disapproved at Stuttgart. But the Duke kept the composer busy during his short stay, after which they proceeded to Weimar where the Grand Duke and his daughter-in-law, Maria Pavlovna, sister of the Tsar, gave them a cordial welcome. It was here that Weber met Goethe, but without deriving much pleasure from the privilege, for the poet had no ears for anyone but Zelter and talked through the music, barely acknowledging the introduction.

Another visit to Dresden, and then the wandering pair turned to Berlin, where they arrived on 20th February, 1812. This first visit to the Prussian capital lasted until 31st August and resulted in several new friendships that were to prove valuable on Weber's return. But his wanderings were not yet over. He again visited Gotha, Weimar and Leipzig, and reached Prague in January, 1813, just as the directorship of the theatre had become vacant. He was appointed to the post with a mission to reorganise the opera, which had sadly deteriorated since the days when Mozart, a generation earlier, had produced there his immortal 'Don Giovanni.' The new duties involved a journey to Vienna in search of artists. On his return he plunged into work. There was no department of the theatre that did not receive his attention, and when he found that his unwelcome diligence was discussed by his subordinates in a language he did not understand, Czech, he promptly learned it. He opened his first season on 10th September, 1813, and retained his post until 30th September, 1816. During those three years much history was made and the map of Europe considerably altered. Commemorative compositions appear in the list of his works, but no operas. He was too much occupied in staging those of other composers.

In his private life, however, there occurred serious developments. Attached to the theatre was a dancer named Brunetti, whose wife, though the mother of several children, still possessed youthful charm. Thinking thereby to gain influence with the director, Brunetti appears to have connived at a liaison which caused the composer much suffering in the end. He was infatuated, but Thérèse Brunetti merely preyed upon him. This, however, did not prevent her from indulging in terrible scenes of jealousy. His diary is evidence of what he went through at this period. Meanwhile he had not forgotten the favourable impression made upon him by Caroline Brandt at the first performance of 'Silvana.' Since then she had made considerable progress on the various opera stages of Germany, and Weber engaged her for Prague. She made her début there on New Year's Day, 1814, in Isouard's 'Cinderella' and reaped an immediate success. His interest in her was at first purely professional but gradually he came to admire her sterling qualities, her modest charm, her discretion and her filial devotion until, whilst still believing himself in love with Thérêse Brunetti, he unconsciously developed a tender regard for Caroline. Needless to say this did not escape the jealous alertness of Mme Brunetti, and there were renewed scenes, but his eyes were opened by her conduct, and he became betrothed to Caroline. The course of true love did not, however, run any smoother than usual, and many misunderstandings intervened before their marriage took place on 4th November, 1817.

Meanwhile he had revisited Berlin during his summer vacation in 1814, produced 'Silvana' there and composed some patriotic songs which stirred the nation. The following year, after the battle of Waterloo, he wrote a cantata, 'Kampf und Sieg,' which was performed at Prague in December, and in Berlin on the first anniversary of the battle, 1816, with great popular success. The post of Kapellmeister in Berlin was then vacant, and he hoped to obtain the appointment, but even the active intervention of his friend Count Brühl, the Intendant, failed at that time to secure it for him. But he was not to remain unattached. On his way to Berlin he had been summoned to Pillnitz, the country palace of King Friedrich August of Saxony, to receive an acknowledgment, in valuable form, of a copy of 'Kampf und Sieg.' It was handed to him on his sovereign's behalf by Count Vitzthum, the King's equerry, whose brother, the Court marshal, was director of the Royal Theatre at Dresden. The latter was then staying at Carlsbad, where his brother persuaded Weber to visit him on his way back. As a result of this meeting he was given in December, 1816, the appointment as conductor of the German Opera at Dresden. He took up his duties there on 13th January, 1817. Less than six months later the Berlin appointment again fell vacant, and this time Count Brühl was in a position to offer it to him. It had some advantages over Dresden, but while Weber was hesitating the decision was placed beyond his power by the burning down of the Berlin theatre. At Dresden, therefore, he remained. On 13th September his appointment was confirmed for life, and in December he brought home his bride.

Dresden and the New Opera

His years of wandering were thus ended. This did not stand in the way of frequent professional visits to Berlin, where efforts continued to be made to induce him to stay, to Prague and Vienna, and subsequently to London, but Dresden became his permanent domicile. His works at that date included, apart from those already named, his two piano concertos and several concert works for other instruments; three of his four piano sonatas and several shorter works for piano; his piano quartet, six violin sonatas, many songs and a large number of occasional pieces.

The position at Dresden was at first somewhat difficult. Whereas in all other musical centres of Central Europe German opera had firmly established itself, in Dresden the Italian tradition so long fostered under the eighteenth-century Electors still remained firmly entrenched. Court Marshal von Vitzthum had succeeded, with difficulty, in inducing the King to sanction the establishment of German opera, but Count Einsiedel, the Prime Minister, was bitterly opposed to it, and to Weber as its protagonist. It had been understood when Weber was appointed that he should rank equally with his Italian colleague, Francesco Morlacchi, but when the appointment came to be gazetted a lower title was given him. The tussle that ensued was symbolical of much that was to follow, but it ended in his favour. Another complication was that the King of Saxony had sided with Napoleon and been punished in the settlement by losing some provinces to Prussia. He was compelled to acquiesce in the new situation, but resented any reference to the past struggle, in which he had been on the wrong side. Weber's patriotic songs thus became counters in the intrigues against him and his popularity in Berlin was reckoned almost a crime. At first Morlacchi and he got on fairly well together, but in these conditions mischief-making was easy and soon became rife. In fact, for a time the Italo-German musical struggle was as acute as the similar conflict in Paris in the eighteenth century. That Weber in the end 'won through' is evidence, not only of his great gifts, but perhaps even more of his tenacity of purpose. Having set his hand to the plough he did not turn back. He did far more than establish German opera in Dresden. He became the founder of romantic German opera, and the precursor of modern music-drama. From the date of his appointment to that of his death was little more than nine years, but the effect of what Weber accomplished in that short time is with us yet.

Der Freischütz

Soon after he had settled in Dresden, Weber had formed a friendship with Friedrich Kind, who, like many a barrister before and since, had deserted the law for literature. The suggestion having naturally arisen that Kind should provide the composer with a libretto, the latter recalled the vivid impression made on him seven years earlier by Apel's story Der Freischütz. They discussed the scenario together on 21st February, 1817, and a week later, on 1st March, the book was ready. Composition, however, proceeded at first slowly, Weber's time being so much occupied with his duties connected with the opera, and with other tasks, notably several compositions for the Court, such as the cantata 'L'Accoglienza' for the marriage of the Princess Maria Anna Carolina of Saxony to the Grand Duke Leopold of Tuscany; a Mass in E flat for the King's name-day; a Jubilee cantata and the well-known Jubilee overture for the 50th anniversary of his accession, and a Mass in G for his golden wedding. He also wrote the incidental music to several plays produced at the Court Theatre. Three of his best-known piano works, the 'Rondo brillante,' the 'Invitation to the Dance,' and the 'Polacca brillante,' also date from this period, as well as the trio for piano, flute and cello, Op. 63, and numerous smaller works. Thus it happened that, although isolated numbers of 'Der Freischütz' were composed in 1817, 1818, and 1819, it was not until the autumn of that year that he was able to work continuously at it, and the overture, which was the last portion to be written, was completed on 13th May, 1820. Meanwhile Count Brühl, who had been unremitting in his efforts on Weber's behalf in Berlin, had pledged himself to produce the opera at the new theatre which Schinkel was constructing to replace the one that had been burned down. But before this took place another dramatic work made its appearance. Count Brühl, being dissatisfied with the incidental music which Traugott Maximilian Eberwein had composed for Wolff's melodrama *Preciosa*, commissioned Weber to write the music for its production in Berlin, which, the new theatre not being ready, took place at the Court Theatre, 14th March, 1821.

More Operas

On 2nd May, 1821, Weber left for Berlin and found himself confronted by a situation resembling in one respect that which he had left behind at Dresden. Spontini had recently been appointed to the Opera. He was favoured by the Court, whose opinions were only too readily adopted by society. His operas 'The Vestal,' 'Cortez' and 'Olympia' had been produced in a spectacular manner, with great success, and the adherents of national opera, though the music of *Preciosa* had aroused their interest in the coming production, were a little despondent concerning its prospects. Weber alone remained unaffected by any such misgivings. On the very morning of the first performance, 18th June, he surprised his wife and his pupil, Julius Benedict, by playing to them a composition he had just completed for piano, and detailed to them its poetic basis. This was the 'Concert-Stück' for piano and orchestra, of which the first idea had occurred to him in Dresden the previous February, but which he had worked at during the last fortnight, and finished that very morning. It was to become one of his most popular compositions. The success of 'Der Freischütz' was never in doubt. At the outset the overture was greeted with such a storm of approval that it had to be repeated before the opera could proceed. The evening ended in triumph. The partisans of national opera were jubilant. The only dissentients were Spohr, who was never responsive to Weber's music, and Zelter, who wrote disparagingly to Goethe, as he so often did on new composers.

In October the opera was produced at Vienna, amid similar scenes, and Barbaja, the astute impresario of the Kärnthnerthor Theatre, promptly commissioned another opera from the same pen. Weber had one in hand, begun before the completion of 'Der Freischütz,' but it was a comic opera, 'The Three Pintos,' on Seidel's novel *Der Brautkampf*, and it would not have been suitable. This work was destined to remain unfinished. A libretto was suggested by Helmina von Chezy, whom Benedict describes as 'a stout elderly lady, with all the qualities of a real blue-stocking, careless and slovenly in her appearance, not blessed with any earthly goods, but with a great deal of self-sufficiency.' She had discovered an old legend: 'Histoire de Gérard de Nevers et de la belle et vertueuse Euryanthe, sa mie.' She submitted two acts which Weber accepted, subject to alteration, and thus was born Weber's penultimate opera 'Euryanthe.' It was completed in August, 1823, and produced at the Kärnthnerthor Theatre on 25th October. The music won him a good reception on the first night, but it was too severely handicapped by its libretto to be an enduring success. Frau von Chezy was no genius, as Schubert was to learn afterwards, when he wrote the incidental music which is all that survives of another of her dramatic works, *Rosamunde*.

England and the End

Meanwhile the success of 'Der Freischütz' had been making operatic history, and it continued to create a furore wherever it was performed. In London it had been presented at three theatres simultaneously, Covent Garden, Drury Lane and the Lyceum, and its popularity induced Charles Kemble to invite the composer to write an opera in English for the first-named theatre. Weber by then was in such a state of health that before accepting he consulted his physician, who declared that unless he went to a warmer climate and rested he gave him no more than a few months to live. But Weber who had known many years of poverty, thought that the profits from the London engagement would enable him to make better provision for his family, and accepted, after Kemble's terms had been raised to £1,000. He set himself to learn English, in which he had 153 lessons from a certain Mr. Carey between 20th October, 1824, and 11th February, 1826, the last being five days before his departure for London. Meanwhile the subject of 'Oberon' had been chosen and J. R. Planché entrusted with the task of writing the libretto, which was sent to the composer early in 1825. He set to work upon it at once, but laid it aside for a time during the summer. He resumed work in the autumn, and in January, 1826, little was needed to complete the opera except the overture, which he added in London, where he arrived on 5th March. He stayed in Great Portland Street at the house of Sir George Smart, whose acquaintance he had made the previous summer at Ems. The first performance of the opera took place on 12th April under the direction of the composer, whose contract stipulated that he should conduct the first twelve. Apart from that he gave several concerts and was kept busy with engagements of all kinds, including many which, in his precarious state of health, might have been spared him. The result was what his Dresden physician had foreseen. The disease from which he suffered was aggravated and he died on 6th June, 1826, not yet forty years old. He was buried at Moorfields Chapel, but in 1844 the coffin was removed to Dresden and reinterred with a ceremonial of which the musical portion was under the direction of Richard Wagner, who spoke an eloquent farewell over the grave.

Not Without Honour

There are some aspects of those last years that call for comment. How came it that, he being a State official at the Saxon capital, his last four dramatic works were produced elsewhere, in Berlin, Vienna and London? The answer is that, as happens often in the case of genius, his immediate environment was the last to learn of his greatness. At Dresden he lived in a world of intrigue and of acrimonious controversy, which belittled him to his fellow townsmen. Some, of course, knew him for what he was, but to many it may never have occurred that a man of whom this and that was said—for slander was rife—could be a genius. Hence he was regarded as a man who performed competently the duties entrusted to him, and little more. This is vividly shown by the remark of the Dresden Intendant, von Lüttichau, who happened to be in Berlin when 'Euryanthe' was performed there for the first time. After a rehearsal he saw a large crowd waiting outside the theatre to catch a glimpse of the composer, and said to him in surprise: 'Weber, are you then really a celebrity?' This was less than six months before Weber's death, at a time when all operatic Europe was acclaiming him.   The attitude explains how Dresden, which could have demanded the privilege of producing his works, allowed them to go elsewhere and followed in the wake of other opera houses.

Limitations of space preclude our dwelling upon the anecdotal side of those later years, on his many friendships in the world of art and letters no less than in that of music, or on his meeting with Beethoven.   Life then was less adventurous than it had been in his youth, but no less full of vital interest.   As with many consumptives, Weber's intellectual activities were in inverse ratio to his constitutional weakness. Like Mozart, Schubert and Mendelssohn he was doomed to die young, but he made history.

BIBLIOGRAPHY

BENEDICT, J.: *Weber.*   2s. 6d.   (Low, 'Great Composers' Series, 1928.)

PENGUIN MUSIC MAGAZINE

EDITED BY RALPH HILL

Issued at three-monthly intervals, Penguin Music Magazine is intended to give the music lover information on the world of music and musicians. The subjects, written by acknowledged authorities, are varied and controversial and each issue contains thirty-two pages of illustrations. A selection from the contents of some previous issues is given below.

Penguin Occasionals

*

PENGUIN NEW WRITING

EDITED BY JOHN LEHMANN

A collection of critical and creative writing. Its contributions are selected from the works of world known writers, artists and new authors. Each issue also contains sixteen pages of plates illustrating new work of the theatre and painting.

PENGUIN PARADE

EDITED BY J. E. MORPURGO

Presents in an invigorating manner informative articles by authoritative writers on social and artistic affairs. The contents are varied, consisting of critical essays on the arts and social problems, short stories, poems and illustrations, both in colour and photogravure, from work by contemporary artists.

NEW BIOLOGY

EDITED BY M. L. JOHNSON AND MICHAEL ABERCROMBIE

A miscellany of essays summarising aspects of contemporary biological research and application. Each number has an inset of plates and a glossary of the scientific terms used in the text.

SCIENCE NEWS

Up-to-date authoritative information on scientists and their work, compiled by experts for the student, teacher and the non-professional reader. Also contains line drawings and plates to illustrate the subjects treated.

PENGUIN FILM REVIEW

EDITED BY R. K. NEILSON BAXTER, ROGER MANVELL AND H. H. WOLLENBERG

A regular publication devoted to up-to-the-minute film news and matters, surveying, in a progressive, stimulating manner, all the activities and influences of the film, economically, socially and aesthetically. Also contains thirty-two pages of illustrations from recent British and foreign films.

THE PENGUIN CLASSICS

A Library of New Translations

EDITED BY E. V. RIEU

IN PREPARATION
From the Greek

From the Latin

From the Spanish

From the French

From the Russian

From the Norwegian

PENGUIN BOOKS LIMITED
London and New York